THE PENN STATE WALK-ON

OVERCOMING THE PAIN AND LEGACY OF SUICIDE
THROUGH FOOTBALL, FAITH, AND FAMILY

SUE AND TIM IORIO

The Penn State Walk-On: Overcoming the Pain and Legacy of Suicide Through Football, Faith, and Family

Copyright © 2020 Sue and Tim Iorio. All rights reserved. No part of this book may be reproduced or retransmitted in any form or by any means without the written permission of the publisher.

Published by TNTSJ Publishing
Scottsdale, Arizona 85254 USA

ISBN: 978-1-0878-5733-6 (paperback)
ISBN: 978-1-0878-5734-3 (ebook)
LCCN: 2019921152

*In memory of
Nick Iorio*

CONTENTS

Acknowledgments vii

Preface ix

1 Lives Changed Forever 1

2 Tragedy Strikes 32

3 The Aftermath 44

4 Coping 56

5 The Light Begins Shining 74

6 An Amazing Time 87

7 The NFL and Beyond 95

8 Mental Health & Gun Safety 105

Conclusion 110

Epilogue 115

ACKNOWLEDGMENTS

There are so many people who were there for us, some silently holding us up, and too many to name. We are forever indebted and want to thank all of them. We especially want to thank our extended family for the many things they did to help us grieve and heal. We also wish to acknowledge some of the people who made this memoir possible.

Tim Iorio, MD – Tim's strong critique and thoughts added to the quality of the stories. He persevered in spite of the tragedy of losing his brother and helped us to focus on his development to become an orthopedic surgeon.

Joe Iorio – Joe shared his ideas and gave us so many good times and cherished memories while playing Penn State football.

Ted Iorio, Esq. – Uncle. He has been a confidant and provided us with ideas and guidance on publishing this memoir.

Ray Miller – Ordained minister and Tim's (Sr.) close

friend. He provided our family with spiritual guidance throughout this journey.

Jay Paterno – Author, former football coach, and son of Coach Joe Paterno. Jay was one of the first contacts who encouraged us to write this memoir. We thank Jay for recommending our son Joe as a preferred walk-on to Coach Paterno.

Paul Levine – A prominent international author and a Penn State Alumnus. Paul, referred to us by Jay Paterno, was so gracious to review our first synopsis. He believed our story to be powerful and recommended that we pursue writing this memoir.

Paul Zucarelli – Author. We met Paul through our church, St. Bernadette, Scottsdale, AZ. Paul gave us many points on writing and publishing a book. He referred us to Wheatmark in Tucson, AZ.

Penn State Arizona Alumni Group – Our friends in Phoenix since 2014 who graduated from Penn State. They encouraged us in writing this memoir. Thank you, friends!

PREFACE

In our wildest imaginations, we never thought we would write a memoir. But, then we never believed we would experience the loss of a child. Particularly the loss of a child to suicide.

When we were starting our family over forty years ago, suicide never crossed our minds. We were so busy working and raising our family we didn't think about such things. Mental illness was stigmatized and suicide wasn't talked about openly in those times.

Things have changed since then. Although there remains a stigma on mental illness, suicide is frequently in the news, be it of a celebrity, a sports figure, someone from the military, or a teenager or child who was bullied at school or through social media. The magnitude of the problem became more evident to us when we recently participated in a local walk for suicide prevention. There were thousands of people who came together to walk in memory of their friends and family members who died from suicide. Similar events are being held every month in cities all over the United States and the world.

We began to reflect on our experience after the

death of our oldest son from suicide. We felt our story might help other suicide survivors learning to live again with the pain. Up until now, we were not able to talk about the use of a gun.

Many stories have come to mind about how we felt and what we did to heal from the loss of Nick. Penn State football was an enormous part of the process. It provided us a tremendous distraction from our suffering. The love of our family and our belief in God gave us the strength to move forward each day. And as time passed, we found we could once again enjoy life.

1

LIVES CHANGED FOREVER

"I measure every grief I meet with narrow probing eyes."
(Emily Dickinson, 1862)

The year 1997, our life as a family was forever changed. Sue, my wife, and I were a happy family, raising three sons, Nick, Tim, and Joe. We embraced the joys and struggles of everyday living until October 28, when we were thrust into a living hell. That was the day our oldest son, Nick, took his life. He was twenty years old and a junior at Bowling Green State University, majoring in Finance in the College of Business Administration with a 4.0 grade point average when he died.

Sue and I met through mutual friends when I was nineteen and she had just turned twenty-one. She was finishing nursing school, and I was a junior in college. Our friends, who knew each other, separately encouraged us to come with them to a local dance place, The Agora. The Agora was just a large room with loud music where soft drinks and beer were sold. The room was dark, lit only by the colored lights on the stage near the dance floor. Song after song, sweaty college students piled on the floor, dancing while music played by a live band filled the room. Sue and I danced to nearly every song, and when we weren't dancing we were engaged in nonstop conversation. An undeniable chemistry kept us focused on each other as if no one else were present in the room. Sue knew that night that we would one day get married.

We dated for a year before becoming engaged. Sue had finished nursing school and started working evenings at one of the hospitals in Toledo. She wanted to continue her schooling, so she eventually left the hospital and began working days for three prominent pediatricians. The change from working evenings to days allowed Sue to go to school after work.

She moved out of the house and into her own apartment. I was still in college living with my grandparents because my parents moved to South Bend, Indiana, for Dad's job. Sue and I didn't live together but I spent a lot of time at her place.

I'll never forget that fall Saturday afternoon while at her apartment when she talked me into looking for an engagement ring. I was engrossed in the Southern Cal versus Notre Dame football game on the TV. She didn't mind if I watched the game as long as we could look at engagement rings. We rushed off to the jewelers at halftime and, before I knew it, picked out a gold ring with a small diamond and gold wedding band. It was all we could afford.

We became engaged that December on the evening of her company's Christmas party. We'll never forget it. We were both nicely dressed for the party, which was being held at the home of one of the pediatricians. Sue's apartment was lit only by the brightly colored lights of her Christmas tree. The weather was cold and a beautiful blanket of freshly fallen snow covered the ground. It was the perfect romantic night. Even though she knew about the ring, I surprised her when I asked her to marry me on that evening.

The following year, I graduated from the University of Toledo with a Bachelor of Arts degree. We married in July, loaded our things into a rental truck, and moved to Champaign, Illinois, where I attended the University of Illinois for graduate school. Sue got a job as a nurse at Burnham City Hospital. For extra income, I drove a truck while going to school full-time. Sue had a few small school loans she needed to pay, and we had my tuition for graduate school. Money was tight considering tuition bills, rent, and a car payment. There were weeks when all we had left to eat before payday was one egg. But we were young, in love, and happy. We had our whole lives ahead of us.

On our first anniversary the next July we celebrated with a big surprise when we learned Sue was pregnant with our first child. Nick was born on February 11, 1977, 7:56 a.m., at Burnham City Hospital in Champaign, Illinois, weighing seven pounds, five ounces. After my graduation from the University of Illinois, we moved back to Toledo. It was so nice to be close to family. Sue's sister, Kay, and my grandmother helped watch Nick while we went to work.

Growing up, Nick was an energetic kid who seemed to love life. He was playful and imaginative.

At three years old, he loved to dress up like me in a three-piece suit he got for Easter. He would drive his pedal car around the house as if going off to work at the office. We called him The Little Senator. When not in his suit, he would wear his plastic cowboy boots plus hat and holster as if he were ready to shoot the bad guys. But his favorite outfit was a football uniform complete with helmet and shoulder pads that he got for Christmas when he was six. Dressed in his uniform, he would take a stance and hike the ball to his brother Tim, imitating what he saw at the many football games we went to or watched on TV. Sports became a big part of his life. But, like me, football was his passion. He couldn't wait until he was in the fifth grade and old enough to play organized ball. He played other sports, including basketball, soccer, and baseball, but nothing compared to his love of football.

Besides sports, Sue and I wanted to expose our children to as many different opportunities as possible so they could determine what they were best at and what they wanted to do with their lives. Realizing that the early years were very important in a child's development, we were fortunate that Sue's profession as a nurse allowed her to work part-time and stay home while the kids were little. She would work either at night or on the weekends while I was at home with the kids. I was climbing the corporate ladder, yet we still had to make sacrifices so we could give them what we believed was the best. It was a lot of work but we enjoyed almost every minute of it.

Nick was a very active three-year-old. We had a

hard time keeping him busy. Sue would read to him, take him to story time at our local library, and enroll him in gymnastics and swimming at the YMCA. Sometimes he would sit at the little table and chairs in our basement family room and pretend he was a talk show host. He would act like he was interviewing a guest, playing both the host and the guest. Being our only child at the time, we felt he needed more socialization with children his age, so we decided to enroll him in a preschool program.

We wanted the very best education we could afford for our children. Fairgreen Preschool was a highly recommended private preschool where the children were taught their colors, numbers, letters, and citizenship and had fun with other children their age. It was held three mornings a week at a nearby church. While the kids were in class, the parents, mostly stay-at-home moms, would get together, have coffee, and listen to an occasional speaker.

Halloween time, the children would come to school dressed in their costumes and walk single file down the sidewalk near the school. The street was busy, and drivers passing by would honk with delight about these little three- and four-year-olds in all sorts of costumes, parading down the street. Nick loved to dress up in different costumes when he was little, so Halloween was always fun for him. That year for Halloween, at age three, he wanted to be the Hulk from his favorite TV show. Because the Hulk was one of the good guys, we didn't have any qualms about Nick dressing like him for Halloween. Sue made a pair of black silk shorts and bought long underwear, dyed it green, and stuffed old newspaper in his arms to resemble muscles. She had an old short brown wig for Nick to wear and painted his face with green face paint to match the dyed underwear. He was thrilled. He would flex his little arms while walking around making a roaring sound. Sue and I laughed at his antics, never thinking he might scare the little girls at school, which he did.

At graduation from preschool, Fairgreen had a darling tradition. Each of the little graduates wore a graduation gown complete with mortarboard and gave a performance to parents and guests. The performance included hand gestures to the words of a song. The little graduates had to remember both the words to the song and the hand movements. When the performance was over, each child would come forward to receive a diploma. Nick, with his mortarboard tipped to one side, was in the front row during the performance. He was not the least bit shy singing loudly while moving his hands in unison to the words of the song. Following the performance, with a big smile across his face and still donned in his yellow graduation gown and mortarboard, he swiftly pranced with confidence across the stage to receive his diploma. He was ready at four years old to go on to prekindergarten.

Ladyfield School was a private catholic grade school run by the Sisters of Notre Dame whose mission was dedicated to educating children. Ladyfield started with prekindergarten K4, then kindergarten, and went until eighth grade.

Acceptance into a catholic school was almost a given if you were a member of the parish. And there was generally very little, if any, tuition because the school was supported by the parish. Entrance into Ladyfield was different. Unlike most catholic grade schools, Ladyfield was unaffiliated with a parish. It had one class per grade, limiting the number of students who were accepted. There was a waiting list to get in. People would put their children on the list as soon as they were born. Because there was no support from a parish, Ladyfield had tuition. With Sue working only part-time while our kids were little, it was difficult at times to pay the tuition; but we felt the quality of the education was worth it.

An important part of the Ladyfield philosophy was an expectation of family involvement. Parents were asked to assist any way they could. In the younger grades, Sue would help once or twice a week by coming to the classroom and listening to kids read. Some parents would help on the playground or in the cafeteria. Together with other parents, we helped to start Cub Scouts. I acted as the first cub master even though I was only a Cub Scout myself. We also helped begin a basketball and soccer program. The teams were able to compete in the Catholic Youth Organization, or CYO as it is known.

Although Ladyfield did not have a football program, Nick, and Joe were able to play CYO football through our parish. By the time Nick was in seventh grade, his CYO team was playing in the final league game, the Toy Bowl. That game, he scored the winning touchdown, and his team won the prestigious event. The seventh grade team's success led to the squad he played on in eighth grade being placed in a higher division. That year, his team did not win one game. Frustrated, Nick wanted to quit. But I told him, "there are no quitters in this family." He reluctantly hung in and finished the season with his team. The experience of going from the championship team to a losing team helped him learn a valuable lesson in life: "Sometimes you will win, but sometimes you will lose."

In grade school, Nick also learned Taekwondo. His interest in martial arts led him to write a small book about it when he was only in third grade. The handwritten book, titled *Karate for Sports and Self-Defense*, contained quotes from me and tips about different types of punches and how to kick and block punches. Nick was a tough kid in Taekwondo. By eighth grade, he earned a yellow belt and was beating adult black belts. The head of the dojo told me he was the "toughest kid in karate" he ever saw. In high school, he became busy with football and wrestling, and, since there was little time for martial arts, he decided to give it up.

Another sport we enjoyed as a family was playing golf. We joined Brandywine Golf Course. The guys and I would play as often as we could during the summer. It was a lot of fun to be with my three boys. Nick was in high school, and Tim and Joe were still in grade school. They were all so competitive, but especially

Nick. Joe was the biggest of the three and had just started puberty, with his voice beginning to change. I remember one time when we were at the third hole at Brandywine. Nick shot one right into the water. Joe, in a high squeaky voice, began to chide him about his shot, and Nick chased him around the hole with his club. Tim just stood by and watched, as he was playing the best of all of them. We shared a lot of time with each other, having fun and talking about life. I am so thankful for those days.

We wanted our kids to be well rounded, so in addition to sports, we exposed them to music, art, and theater. We would frequently visit the Toledo Art Museum, go to plays at the theater, and offer each of them the opportunity to learn a musical instrument. We thought that maybe one of them might take to playing an instrument, even though neither of us did. Sue took piano as a young girl for a short time. I tried to teach myself the drums. Sue's father could play the organ, and my grandmother taught herself how to play the piano.

Nick was the first to take music lessons, deciding at age nine to learn piano. Later, Tim took piano lessons too. He eventually even taught himself to play guitar. Joe wanted to play the saxophone.

We didn't have a lot of money so we bought an inexpensive but sturdy old upright piano that at one time had been a player piano. The only remnants from its early days were its disconnected pedals protruding beneath the slot where rolls for the music were once housed. All its keys worked so we had it tuned. Both

Nick and Tim used it to practice their lessons, and my grandmother would play it when she came to visit. Thankfully, for Joe's lessons, Sue's parents lent us her brother's saxophone. Joe and the horn only lasted two weeks.

Nick and the piano didn't last too long either. His teacher, a well-groomed middle-aged woman who taught children's lessons from her home, told us that she wasn't sure piano was the best instrument for Nick. But we all agreed for him to give it a try for at least a year.

His first and only performance was held at the Stranahan Family's historic home in Toledo, Ohio. Founders of Champion Spark Plugs, the Stranahan Family was once among the most prominent families in Ohio. When they left Toledo, their expansive estate was donated to the county and developed into The Wildwood Park. On the estate grounds sat the Stranahan mansion. The large brick home had several rooms where the elite from the area once held elaborate balls and parties. The concert for the young piano students was held in the mansion's ballroom. Several high arched windows angled along the ballroom forming small alcoves. A shiny black piano was located in one of the alcoves, near the front of the room. Sunlight from the warm Sunday afternoon filtered into the alcove, brightening the area for each performer. Nick, dressed in a dark blue sport coat, white shirt, tie, and dress pants with black dress shoes, sat smartly on the bench when it was his turn to play. His feet barely touched the piano pedals as he began to play the simple little songs we heard him practice over and over on the old player piano. Finishing his performance, he slid from the bench, stood proudly, and took a bow, ending his piano lessons.

Nick's imaginative personality once again surfaced in the eighth grade. Every Christmas, Ladyfield would hold an annual Christmas musical. The play always ended with a scene from the birth of Christ in the manger with a live baby playing Christ and including the entire student body. It was considered one of the special events for eighth grade students, signifying a rite of passage because the students played the lead characters. The middle-grade students typically stood on bleachers acting as the chorus. The youngest students often stole the show. Dressed in cute homemade costumes, dancing and singing innocently on stage, one or two would be out of sync and staring into the audience. Trying to find a play to include kids as young as four and as old as thirteen was always a challenge for the music teacher. Sometimes the plots were a little unusual.

Nick really wanted to play the part of Scrooge for the Christmas musical. We had gone to see the play *A Christmas Carol* a few years before, and he never forgot it. Upon his urging, the music teacher was able to obtain its copyright, and it was decided *A Christmas Carol* would be that year's play. Nick was so excited. He memorized the lines for Scrooge in one day on the bus coming home from school. He went to the library and got as many taped versions of the play as he could, watching them over and over again. Viewing the tapes, he studied every mannerism of Scrooge's character. He even used an English accent while trying out for the part. His hard work landed him the part of Scrooge. The entire eighth grade class performed the play with gusto. It was long remembered as the best Ladyfield Christmas play ever.

Nick graduated from Ladyfield in 1991 with high honors. The following fall he entered St. Francis de Sales High School. St. Francis is one of two all-boy college-prep high schools in Toledo, Ohio, run by the Oblate priests. The other all-boy school in town is their rival, St. John's Jesuit High School.

All summer, Nick worked out, getting ready to play football for St. Francis. He couldn't wait to start freshman football. His new nickname was "Rocky," like the movie about the Philadelphia boxer. In the movie, Sylvester Stallone plays an underdog boxer who defeats his opponent to become the champion. Like Rocky, while running outside, Nick would wear a gray sweatshirt and pants with a black stocking cap. Occasionally, he would stop in the street and pretend to throw a few punches in the air just like the character in the movie. His summer workouts paid off when it was time for St. Francis freshman football. He was well built, a solid 165 pounds, and five feet, ten inches tall. He was picked to play both center and linebacker. But for the biggest game of his freshman season against rival St. John's, he was disappointed because he was not allowed to play. The head coach had called to tell me he was suspended for fighting in the locker room. My only comment to the coach was, "If he deserved it, then go through with it." Nick never did that again.

We did notice that Nick seemed to have trouble adjusting to the change from grade school to high school. His close friends from grade school chose not to go to St. Francis, so it meant he had to make new friends. He seemed quieter and didn't talk about any new friends. Every night after football practice, he would come home carrying all his books from his classes. He was isolated in his room, studying most evenings and on the weekends. We knew St. Francis was a rigorous school, but we soon learned Nick's academic achievement demonstrated his intellect.

At the end of the first quarter, the freshman honors program was held in the high school gym. Parents and guests sat on folding chairs in the middle of the gym, which was also used for indoor sports like wrestling and basketball. A large scoreboard hung at one side of the room and banners from former city league and state championship games were displayed along the walls. The faint smell from past sporting events and 200 or so freshman teenage boys hung in the air. The students, dressed in the school uniform of sport coats with ties, sat on bleachers lining the brick walls that gleamed with the school colors of red and blue. A table with the teachers sitting in a row and a microphone and podium were at the front of the room, where the principal—who was also a priest—stood. The program began, and one by one the priest called each student's name and grade point average, starting with the lowest number first.

We thought Nick might be in the Top 10, but we did not expect what was about to happen next. The final students' names were called. Nervously, we listened for his call; after nine students were listed, there was no sign of Nick. All of a sudden we heard, "and at number one, Nicolas Iorio." As humble as he was, he never told us he was number one. His football teammates, including those playing varsity, could not believe that this tough kid had achieved number-one status.

In the summer of 1992, Nick was again working out extremely hard, preparing for his sophomore football season. He had hopes of being the backup center for the varsity football team in the fall. I would stop by the field occasionally to watch him practice. Ohio summers, especially July and August, are hot and muggy, making it tougher on the players in full pads, preparing for the season. As I focused on Nick during double sessions in the unrelenting August heat, I could see the sweat pouring down his face. He was giving it his all, as he always did. His workouts paid off. He made second-team center on the varsity team as a sophomore.

What was unbelievable was, while Nick was practicing football in the intense summer heat, he also entered a triathlon that summer held in Sylvania. It was the biggest one held in Northwest Ohio. The triathlon included a 10K run, a grueling one-mile swim in the open water of Sylvania's Olander Park Lake, and a twenty-five-mile bike ride. We didn't have a racing bike. Instead, Nick rode an older five-speed bike, making the twenty-five-mile ride in heavy Ohio winds much more difficult. It was the first triathlon Nick had ever participated in. He finished in the top tier for his age group (fifteen years old). His football coaches were at a loss for words when they found out he achieved such a feat while at the same time trying to prepare for the football season.

The most memorable experience from Nick's sophomore season was during the St. John's game. The game was held under the lights at the University of Toledo stadium in front of more than 10,000 people. The October night sky was clear, and the air was cool, perfect for a high school football game. The stadium was electrified with excitement as the schools' pep bands played. Fans cheered while the St. Francis Knights's colors of red and blue and the blue and gold of the St. John Titans could be seen everywhere in the stands. The game was a big one. The winner would be in the lead for the city championship with the potential to go to the state playoffs.

My parents, brother, and sister came to the game. Nick's brothers, Tim and Joe, were there. Sue, just released from the hospital after having surgery and against her doctor's wishes, insisted on attending the game. She was glad she did because the first-team center went down, and Nick was called into action. He played outstandingly well. His assignment was to block a six-feet-four, 275-pound future All-American defensive tackle, who later received a full ride to Northwestern. Nick did a fantastic job blocking him, allowing our backs to go up the middle gaining tons of yardage. St. Francis won the game 21-0. The entire offensive line, including Nick, received Players of the Week honors by the local television station. It was exhilarating.

Nick continued to enjoy playing football throughout high school. By the time his junior year came, he was the starting center on a good team with potential for the city championship. And they won the city championship title, but their hopes for a state title were dashed when they just missed the playoffs. Personally, Nick had a successful season, receiving the second-team all-city award for his play as center. And he finally received his varsity letter.

Immediately after the season, he started preparing for his senior year. Each morning he would work out with weights and then he would run two or three miles. He continued what I used to call his Rocky workouts. Placing a long piece of wood on his shoulders, he would do squats across the yard until it hurt. Alternatively, he would jump up on a pull-up bar, lifting himself up. I watched in amazement, thinking to myself, this kid is getting ready for some serious football. He grew to six feet tall and 215 pounds with a six-pack, developing pectoral muscles and solid arms just like his idol "Rocky."

Senior year football, Nick was co-captain of the team and as tough as nails, playing both center and linebacker. In many of the games, the backs would go up the middle, just like his sophomore and junior years, to gain huge amounts of yardage. In his role as a linebacker, his hits were heard from the stands. These are two of the hardest positions on the field. I wasn't happy that the coaches had him playing both ways, but Nick would say, "I gotta do it for the team."

Ohio has always been a powerhouse for high school football, especially in Division I. That year the competition was especially stiff for St. Francis with two of the best teams in the state, and even the nation, Cleveland St. Ignatius and Lima Senior, competing in their division. St. Francis's season ended in disappointment when their starting quarterback was injured and they began to struggle. They fell short of winning the city championship and making the playoffs. That is football.

Nick was named second-team All-City Center for football. He narrowly missed first-team All-City Center. He really wanted to be All-City in a sport his senior year, so he decided he would wrestle again and hope to take All-City in wrestling. It wouldn't be easy because he hadn't participated in that since the first time wrestling when he was a freshman. He weighed 215 pounds but he would sometimes wrestle as a heavyweight, a sixty-pound difference at 275 pounds. What he lacked in weight and experience, he made up with determination, intelligence, and strength.

Often in the Toledo City high school wrestling matches, the crowd dwindled by the time the last few matches were up. But Nick was such an exciting wrestler to watch that the gym was still full by the time the heavyweight match came to the mat. There are three instances that I clearly remember where he was a true crowd-pleaser. The first instance occurred when, unbeknownst to Nick, he was competing with the number one high school 215-pound wrestler in the nation. He barely lost the match, giving the guy the competition of a lifetime. Nick was upset to learn from his wrestling coach after the match of the guy's wrestling status. He said, "I would have wrestled a different kind of match." The second instance happened when he wrestled in a tournament against Ohio's heavyweight state champ. Nick weighed in at 215 pounds but his opponent was a monster of a kid, every bit of 275 pounds with not one ounce of body fat. Many of the fans in the stands were rooting for Nick, chanting, "Nick, Nick, Nick…" It reminded me of the fans shouting in the *Rocky* movie. Nick lost 6 to 4, but not without wrestling one heck of an exciting match.

The third instance occurred when Nick beat a rival from another catholic school in the city league on his eighteenth birthday. That win earned him All-City honors in wrestling, just as he had hoped.

Following completion of the city league wrestling, Nick progressed to the sectionals, and he took third place. Then he went to the districts, but by then his stamina had changed. When he wrestled, he was gasping for air after only a few minutes. It was frightening to watch his face turn blue while he was struggling to breathe. The referee stopped the match so he could take a break and his color returned to normal. He finished the match but we knew something was wrong, plus he injured his ankle. Later that week, we got him in to see the doctor and learned he had exercise-induced asthma. Although he could continue to wrestle with the help of an inhaler, he decided he was done with that activity.

Nick continued to develop, becoming more comfortable socially throughout high school. He was having fun with sports and made many new friends. After school he was involved in extracurricular activities, and on weekends he was going to parties and school dances. Occasionally, he would go out on a date but nothing was serious. He had several girls as friends and was particularly close to a girl in the neighborhood. He took her to homecoming when they were both sophomores. They remained friends the rest of his life.

For a teenage guy, Nick had a lot of concern and compassion for people. One instance, reminding me how he was way beyond his years, was how he handled his good friend whose father was gay. His friend was struggling with it. Nick tried to help his friend accept his father's lifestyle. He told me that it shouldn't matter to anyone. I agreed with him. After Nick died, his friend's mother told us how thankful she was for Nick's friendship with her son. Tragically, her son died two years after Nick in an auto accident where he was drinking and driving. She told us at his funeral that he never got over Nick's death. He is buried in the same cemetery, just a few rows from Nick.

Another time when I witnessed his compassion occurred when Nick and I went to visit my uncle, my godfather, in the hospital. He was dying of lung cancer. We had plans to play golf at the golf course across from the hospital after our visit. Nick said he wasn't comfortable playing golf after seeing Uncle Jim in the hospital near death. "Dad, I don't think we should play golf out of respect for Uncle Jim," he said to me. We did play golf, but he had me thinking about it. I think he was right.

August 1994, just two weeks before Nick's senior year in high school, a friend and classmate was killed in a car accident. Nick was very upset over his death. We had a long talk about it. I told him that we will never know why it had to happen to him. Although he wasn't as close to him in high school, Nick knew him and his family well. They lived in Sylvania and attended our church. When the boys were younger, they played little league baseball and soccer together. Sue and I, too, felt terribly sad for his parents and siblings. Together with Nick, we attended his funeral. At the Mass, I prayed a silent prayer: *Please God, may I never lose a child.* How was I to know that three years later we would lose our child, Nick? We became close to his friend's parents, sharing a journey no one wants to share. Nick is buried near his friend's grave. We often stop to visit both.

Nick enjoyed going to high school. His junior year, he would get up early every morning and leave for school before his brothers were barely out of bed. He was attending Mass every day. He and I had long talks about life. He was always hard on himself; at times he was driven to a fault. I shared with him that the road is long and narrow; however, also that we must forgive ourselves. I thought he might become a priest. It was interesting because his eighth grade teacher at Ladyfield also thought he might become a priest. And after he died, Father Sanford, an Oblate from St. Francis, told us Nick was talking to him about thoughts of the priesthood. Nick never discussed it with me.

Academically, Nick was seventh in the class by his junior year, excelling in all subjects with a 4.0-plus grade-point average. He had straight As in regular classes and received extra points for AP courses. Learning to think critically, he had good insight for a teenager. A favorite course of his was psychology. The major assignment for his psychology class was to conduct an experiment that involved human behavior. Nick decided he would test how people respond when confronted with someone trying to steal another person's property.

He arranged for a friend to act as a collaborator helping him with his experiment. Ohio weather in late September is usually still warm, so they set up the experiment outside at a local park. It was around 3:00 p.m. on a weekday and the park was busy with students after school and mothers and their children enjoying a beautiful fall afternoon. Nick's plan was to ask at least three different individuals if they would watch his radio for a short time while he went to retrieve something from his car. If they agreed, his friend would come along, try to take the radio, and run off. Instead of going to his car, Nick was actually hidden from view, using our family camera to record the encounter. He wanted to see the reaction of the person whom he asked to safeguard his radio. He believed that most people would feel responsible for the property if they had agreed to safeguard it and that they would attempt to stop the thief. He tested his theory with three different subjects. When his friend returned with the radio, Nick would appear and explain to the participants what just happened. Obtaining the subjects' permission, he would interview them, asking about their response to the thief and what they felt during the episode. At the conclusion of the experiment, Nick explained what he found and whether his theory was supported. All the subjects were women, which he described as a limitation of the study. Nick's teacher was impressed with his experiment, telling him it was the best high school psychology experiment he had seen in his twenty-five years of teaching. He told Nick he was going to use it as a benchmark for his future students.

Another example of Nick's insight became evident when he was seventeen years old. He was applying to various colleges, including Harvard. A requirement for admission was an interview by a Harvard alumnus. In the interview, he was asked a question: "What is your generation's greatest challenge or concern?" Nick didn't believe he did a good job answering the question. After thinking about it, he wrote an article with his answer to the question. The article, titled "Whatever Feels Good Is Good? Not Necessarily...," was published in *The Catholic Chronicle* in the spring of 1995. Though written over twenty-four years ago, his thoughts remain relevant today for teenagers and young adults. Here is an excerpt from the article:

> It has occurred to me that my generation has serious concern about one of the major philosophies held by many teenagers and young adults: "Whatever feels good is good."
>
> The problem with this way of thinking is demonstrated in many tangible ways. Recently I have noticed more people my age using drugs, especially marijuana. At one time in my life, drugs were considered taboo, and I knew almost no one who used them. I know I have grown and have been exposed to new people, but I have noticed in the last year that a large number of students my age are buying, selling, and using drugs.
>
> Drug use doesn't scare anyone anymore; it is as popular an activity as drinking beer and having sex. These activities are very exciting to more teens because, obviously, they seem to feel good....
>
> I understand that peer pressure and drugs, alcohol, sex, etc. are not new to teens, and my generation is not the first to experiment. What concerns me, however, about the philosophy of doing what it takes to feel good and be accepted is that fewer and fewer people are considering consequences.

> Today, more than ever, those consequences could mean death: death from AIDS, death from drunk driving, death from abortion, and death from suicide...

Reading it now makes us wonder if he was struggling with the peer pressure of using drugs and having sex.

At his graduation from high school, Nick received the athlete award and the Oblate Award for overall top student in his class, the highest honor bestowed to a senior.

He didn't get into Harvard, but he was okay with that. His real dream was to go to Notre Dame University in South Bend, Indiana, and play football. He wasn't being recruited to play at Notre Dame because he was considered too small for Division I football. He figured he could live in South Bend with my mom and dad and try to walk on. When he applied to Notre Dame, he was placed on the waiting list. His acceptance was deferred to the following year. Disappointed, he decided to attend John Carroll University, a Division III Jesuit University in Cleveland, Ohio, a school where he was accepted among many other schools. He received a scholarship of $10,000 per year and planned to play football. At John Carroll, he played football as a center.

His freshman year, he met a girl at John Carroll whom he cared for a lot. She was a very pretty and popular girl. Nick talked to Sue about her. It was the first time he had a heart-to-heart talk with his mom about a girl. Sue remembers him sharing with her how much he cared for her and asking Sue for advice about whether he should tell her how he felt. He did tell her, but she wasn't interested in him. It broke his heart, but he did move past it, dating a couple of other girls later on.

During the summers between his college years, Nick would come home and work to earn spending money. We paid his tuition for college and gave him an older white Chevy truck to drive. He needed money for gas and going out with friends. He saved what he could so he would have money to last throughout the school year. Whatever money he made in the summer was his spending money.

The summer before college, he wasn't able to work because he had knee surgery from a high-school football injury. Early in the summer, after his freshman year of college, his first job was working as a delivery driver for an ice company. The company was near our house, and every once in a while between deliveries he would stop home to say hello and show off his truck. He was so proud of his uniform and the big ice truck he drove. Unfortunately, that job didn't last too long because they no longer needed him. So he found a different job at a popular local Italian deli. He worked behind the counter waiting on customers. Sometimes relatives would stop in. Nick gave them extra-special treatment. Like his Grandpa Iorio, he was always outgoing, carrying on, and joking with them. Here was this smart, good looking, muscular college guy in his white hat and apron, cutting meat and cheese, making everyone laugh and feel at home. The customers loved him.

He began dating a girl from Toledo whom he knew in high school. She was a pretty girl with dark hair. She lived with her mother and younger brother in Toledo. Her father died of suicide a few years earlier. We didn't know it, but he was frequently driving back and forth from John Carroll to Toledo so he could see her. She had dated a few of the guys a year older than Nick in high school and had a reputation of getting around. Nick really liked her, so we accepted his choice.

By the time Nick finished his sophomore year of football at John Carroll in 1996, we began to notice another change in his personality. He seemed depressed. He broke up with his girlfriend, and he wanted to quit the football team. I drove to Cleveland so Nick and I could meet with the head coach to let him know he was quitting the team. The coach pulled me aside and expressed concern over Nick's emotional stability. When we returned home from Cleveland, we had Nick evaluated by a psychiatrist who confirmed our worst fear. He was diagnosed with a mental health disorder, bipolar disease. He began seeing a therapist and eventually was put on a combination of medications, including Klonopin and Prozac.

Nick told us he didn't feel comfortable at John Carroll and wanted to transfer. He decided on Bowling Green State University about twenty minutes from our home. His transfer to BG was completed in time for the spring semester. We felt Bowling Green was a good choice. Being closer to home made it easier for us to keep a close eye on him, and for him it was easier to see his doctor and therapist regularly.

He began the second semester of his sophomore year at Bowling Green State University in January 1997. At first, the change from John Carroll to Bowling Green was difficult for him. He came back and forth frequently from BG to our home. One night, Tim and Joe came into our room and woke us up, telling us Nick had come home and told them he put a hose in his truck's tailpipe in an unsuccessful attempt to take his life. We jumped out of bed, found Nick, and immediately took him to the hospital where he was admitted to the psychiatric ward. He was in the hospital for a few weeks while they adjusted his medication.

By March, he looked very thin. We were worried about him, but we tried to keep everything as normal as possible, telling only a few people of his illness. We had a spring break trip to the beach planned with Tim, Joe, and a few of their buddies. Nick didn't come because his spring break was at a different time, and he didn't want to miss his classes. We didn't want to leave town without someone checking in on him. The only family we told about his illness was my sister Margie. She agreed to have him over for dinner while we were out of town. She too was surprised to see how thin he was. Thankfully, everything worked out while we were gone.

As the semester continued, he seemed to be doing better. Surprisingly, he was doing well in his classes. He needed to do an internship for his finance major, so he secured a summer job at a local bank. The good news was it was a paid internship.

That summer, Nick gained some weight and began to look and act more like his old self. Besides work, he had an active social life. He was dating the same girl from Toledo, on again off again, and he and his best friend, who lived across the street, would go swimming at the quarry during their days off. At night, they frequented the bars in downtown Bowling Green. One hot summer night, Nick and his friend went to Bowling Green for the evening. It was late when they came home. Sue and I were already in bed. His friend woke us up to tell us Nick was beaten up in a bar fight. We ran downstairs and were aghast when we saw him. His face was swollen and bruised. The whites of his eyes were bloodshot with black and blue marks around them, especially near his right temple. There were bruises and scrapes all over his arms and chest. Nick was a tough kid, but several guys were too many for him to fend off. The story his friend told us was he tried to take down a poster at one of the bars in BG. The bar's bouncer and at least four or five other guys jumped him, knocking him to the ground. While on the ground, they kept kicking him in the face and head. Nick never lost consciousness, but we felt he should be evaluated at the emergency room. Despite our urging, Nick refused to go to the hospital. Sue stayed up that night to make sure Nick did not fall into unconsciousness. We did seek the help of an attorney to determine if there was criminal activity with how

Nick was treated by the bouncer. But the attorney believed that, unless Nick's injuries were more serious, he would not have a claim, so we decided to let it go. We always wondered if he suffered a concussion from the repeated blows to his head.

With the beginning of his junior year, Nick found an apartment he could rent with a couple of other guys. It seemed he was settled into the change of schools, living in an apartment and busy with classes. He even pledged a fraternity. But he still missed playing football. Because BG was only twenty minutes from our home, he was able to accept a volunteer position as an assistant varsity football coach with his high school, St. Francis. Tim and Joe were both on the team. It was Tim's senior year at St. Francis. He was playing soccer, but he always wanted to try football. Much to the dislike of his soccer coach, he played football as the punter and kicker. Slender and fast, with a great foot from his years of playing soccer, he was perfect for the position.

Joe, a junior, was six-foot-three, weighing 255. He was playing center and defensive tackle. The team was one of the best St. Francis ever had, ranked seventh in the state with a 10-2 record. I played football at St. Francis in 1970, graduating in 1971. Having all three of my sons on the same team for my alma mater was a dream come true.

Nick was an outstanding coach at St. Francis at both the junior varsity and varsity level. He coached the offensive line and linebackers for the JVs. He influence left an impact on the players. My brother and I went to a JV practice when Nick was steering one of the juniors who was a linebacker. Usually juniors play on the varsity team, but he wasn't ready. He did make the varsity team his senior year and was voted All-City that year. He told me Nick was his inspiration and remains so today. He was the first recipient of the Nick Iorio Scholarship in 1997, set up by Sue and me after Nick's death. The scholarship, in memory of Nick, is given every year after the football season to a junior at St. Francis who exemplifies Nick's hard work and determination. It is to be used toward senior year tuition.

Nick also helped coach the offensive line for the varsity team. Nick was intelligent and an outstanding lineman at center when he played in high school and college. He knew the techniques. Nick would get frustrated with the coach of the line. They were often at odds with one another. I advised him to try to work it out with the coach, but if necessary, he might have to go to the head coach. When Nick died, many of the players, especially the offensive linemen, said he was such an inspirational coach. Several parents of the players wrote us letters telling us what a motivational spirit he was.

Nick coached his brothers too. A big reason Tim went out for the team as a kicker and punter while also playing varsity soccer was because of Nick. In an article for *The Toledo Blade* after we lost Nick, Tim discussed Nick's challenge to him to go out for football.

And then there was Joe, whom Nick would be particularly hard on. Joe would get mad back, go out on the field, and kick butt. When Tim and Joe played basketball with Nick in pickup games at our home, the competition was fierce. I would watch Nick pound Joe, and he would take it. Except one afternoon, Joe gave it back to Nick, pushing him backwards. I couldn't believe what I was seeing. Nick said to him, "See, you can be tough as nails and can perform that way on the field. If you work hard, you use your God-given gift, you could play football at a Notre Dame or Penn State." Joe was a gifted athlete not only in football, but also in track and field, basketball, and even wrestling. He was recruited for track at Penn University, but he was destined to play football for Penn State in memory of Nick.

2

TRAGEDY STRIKES

"A club I never wanted to join"
(*Harvard Public Health* magazine, p. 15, Spring 2013)

Though things seemed to be better, there still were ups and downs for Nick. Late one Friday afternoon, just before a big nighttime St. Francis football game against Central Catholic, I received an emergency phone call from one of Nick's closest friends. He told me that Nick was spaced out. He was walking on West Bancroft Street near the University of Toledo where I went to college, not far from St. Francis and just down from Ottawa Park, a large wooded site. I immediately left the office and drove to West Bancroft Street. When I got there, I found Nick walking aimlessly on the sidewalk. The same sidewalk I used to walk down when I was going to nightclubs during college. It felt like I was in a nightmare. I approached Nick and asked him, "What is going on?" Answering in a slow, slurred speech, he said, "I am all right."

Fearing Nick might walk into traffic, his friend also called the police after he called me. A few minutes later they arrived with a rescue squad. I tried to coax Nick to get into the rescue vehicle, but he refused. "I have my legal rights," he shouted. "No, this is a medical issue," I responded. Finally, after my persistent pleading, he joined the rescue squad. He was taken to the Toledo Hospital emergency room, which is on the other side of Ottawa Park. I remember thinking, *Thank you, Lord. It is going to be okay.*

Sue was just getting home from work when I called her from the hospital. She rushed over to the emergency room, and we met in the waiting area. We went in together to see Nick, but they would only allow us there for a few minutes. Lying on a hospital bed, he was confined with leather wrist restraints. He had an IV in his arm and a heart monitor on that was beeping rapidly in sequence with every heartbeat. They were waiting for the cardiologist to finish seeing him before they moved him upstairs to the psychiatric unit.

The cardiologist was someone we knew from St. Francis. He graduated a few years before me, and his son was on the football team. He told us they were monitoring Nick's heartrate closely because it was very fast. He believed Nick had been taking his Klonopin incorrectly, which was spiking his heart rate and making him very agitated. That explained why he was restrained.

We only spoke to Nick for a few minutes. He wasn't acting like our son. His eyes looked wild. He didn't seem to know who we were. We were told to return to the waiting room. Anxiously sitting there, we suddenly overheard a commotion coming from the direction of Nick's cubicle. Several people, including security guards with keys jangling from their waists, male aids, and nurses in various colored scrubs and white shoes, were running down the hall toward the open emergency room doors. There was such a ruckus that Sue and I ran unnoticed into Nick's room, only to find his bed was empty. The heart monitor, still turned on, was blaring an alarm, and the IV tubing was dangling from the bag hanging from the pole. But Nick was nowhere in sight.

Confused, we cornered the young and attractive nurse who had been tending to Nick. When we asked her what was happening and where was our son, her response horrified us. "Well, I couldn't be with him every minute. I have sicker patients to take care of."

Sue, being a nurse, was so angry that a fellow nurse would say such a thing to us. Nick was as sick as any patient in the ER. His illness was just as lethal as any physical illness. And as his parents, we were just as concerned about our son as any other family was for their relative in the ER. Unfortunately, many healthcare professionals do not understand mental health disorders and some lack compassion for patients with such illnesses. This nurse was one of them. She treated Nick as if he could control what was happening to him. She is part of the problem with why there is a stigma in society for people with mental health disorders.

Nick had jumped off the hospital bed, removed the leather restraints, pulled out his IV, ripped off the leads to the heart monitor, and ran out of the emergency room and into the park. When I realized what happened, I ran after Nick. Finding him in the park, I tried to tackle him. He was too strong for me. The police came shortly thereafter. Together we were able to restrain him, putting him back into a squad car. They took him back to the hospital emergency room, holding him until a bed was ready in the psychiatric ward.

After a few hours, Nick was finally admitted to the psychiatric ward. By then it was evening. We felt the need to support Tim and Joe at the St. Francis versus Central Catholic football game. They had no idea of the ordeal we had just been through with their brother. So we decided to go on to the game. When we arrived at the stadium, St. Francis's head coach looked up, finding us in the stands. We gave him a thumbs-up because we wanted him to know everything was under control. He heard about the incident from St. Francis's president, Father Olszewski or Father "O" as we called him.

Exhausted and weary following the game, we returned to the hospital to check on Nick. It was difficult to believe that our son was going through this. We were both sad and scared for him.

Nick was in a room on the eighth-floor psych unit with adults and adolescents together. When we saw him, we both felt he looked bad. His face was drawn, his skin was pale, and he looked tired but calmer. We told him how much we loved him and that we would return the next day to visit him. The nurse on the unit told us to go home and get some rest and that there was nothing more at this time that could be done for him.

The following day, Nick began undergoing counseling sessions, which included group therapy. There were adults who were chronically ill in the group, some of whom had been in and out of the psych unit. We found it disturbing that a twenty-year-old, a relatively healthy college student, would be in the same group therapy sessions with adults who were chronically ill.

Nick later told us that he learned in the group that he could get disability because of his mental health disorder. He also told his friend they were talking in the group about how to commit suicide by using a gun. Somebody even explained to Nick where to position the gun in his mouth so as not to miss.

After hearing this, we knew it was a mistake for first-time adolescents and young adults to be mixed with more mature chronically ill adults. But that is the way young adults were treated in 1997. Even though Nick was twenty years old and considered by law as an adult, he was not an independent adult. We were still supporting him. He wasn't incompetent, but he also wasn't mature—especially now that he was ill. Our thoughts have since been confirmed by recent scientific studies involving the part of the brain responsible for judgment and decision-making, known as the frontal lobe. In adolescents and young adults, particularly young males, the frontal lobe is still developing. There are even warnings about certain psychiatric medications, including Prozac, causing an increased risk of suicide in adolescents and young adults. Today, teens and adolescents are rarely mixed with older adults.

We continued to question: "When would Nick get healthy again?" "Why Nick?" We had a little hope after talking with his doctor. He believed Nick was what is known as a "Rapid Cycler," meaning his mood could swing very quickly and often from high to low. However, we discovered through his friend, whom Nick had confided in, that he was not taking his medication correctly. He did not like being dependent on it and was trying to get off it by himself. He would stop the Klonopin abruptly, then he would crash. To offset the negative effect of crashing, he would take twice as much. He would repeat the cycle over and over. In essence, he was self-medicating.

Nick only stayed in the hospital about a week. Our insurance was pressuring the doctor to discharge him. Plus, he really didn't like being there and wanted to return to his classes. He convinced his doctor he was fine. We weren't so anxious for him to be discharged, but it was not within our control. We did work out a plan with Nick and his doctor to help him take his medication correctly. Because Klonopin is a controlled substance, once the prescription is filled it can't be refilled until the proper length of time has passed for the amount prescribed. Sue went to the pharmacy and paid for his prescription, giving him what he needed for the week. Then he would come home, and she would give him enough for the next week. The plan did work for a little while.

At first Nick was doing better after getting out of the hospital. All seemed to be going well, and we were having so much fun. The football team was getting ready for the big showdown the next week with their archrival, St. John's High School, for all of the marbles: the city league championship and a trip to the playoffs.

The varsity soccer team was about to play St. John's in the district finals for the first time ever, and St. Francis beat them (Saturday, October 25, 1997). The game was played at Perrysburg High School's field, located just off I-75 highway between BGSU and our home in Sylvania. Lois, Sue's mom, came with us to the game. She loved following the guys' sporting events, coming to games whenever she could. We were surprised when Nick came to watch the game, too. Sue was especially surprised when she saw him dressed only in a lightweight jacket. It was late October, and the weather had already turned cold. The cold weather didn't seem to faze him, though, because his brother Tim was one of the standouts in the game. When the clock ran down to zero, Nick ran out onto the field and tackled him. It was fun to watch the two brothers together, reveling in the victory.

The following day, on Sunday, October 26, we were all home, including Nick, celebrating the big soccer win. Sue decided to make a big dinner so we could all sit down together and eat before Nick headed back to school. Outside the air was crisp and cold with the sounds of leaves rustling in the air as the fall wind blew. The furnace kicked on to keep the house warm from the chill, and the aroma of turkey and dressing baking in the oven filled the house. Nick took a long nap before a good old-fashioned Sunday afternoon dinner. Sue went upstairs to his room to wake him up for dinner so he could eat and head back to school. She told me later that Nick squeezed and hugged her like he had never hugged her before. He told her, "I love you." She will always remember that as the last time he said that to her. After we ate dinner, he left for school. Later that evening, he called to tell me that he had forgotten his wallet. I said, "That's OK. It's at home and you can pick it up tomorrow."

Monday afternoon, Nick stopped at home to get his wallet. Sue and I weren't home from work yet. We learned later that he also stopped at the pharmacy to get a medication refill. Then he drove up to the family cottage in Michigan about an hour away. Before he took off, he left me a phone message, saying he wasn't a timid soul and he was fighting, but he was tired and couldn't take it anymore. The message went on to say, "Don't try to find me." I quickly called Sue at work. We knew from his message he was in trouble. We both immediately left work to drive home. I was out of town at a plant in Indiana. My drive was about an hour long to our house. On the way home, I called my good friend Ray Miller and asked him to pray for us. Sue's job was also about an hour's drive from our home. We both drove as fast as we could to get home, all the while not sure what we would find when we got there.

Once home, we discovered a suicide note from Nick addressed to all of us. The note had small phrases for each of us. To Mom, "I love you"; to Dad, "I am so sorry"; to Tim, "You will be successful"; and to Joe, "Beat the Johnnies." His note, similar to his phone message to me, paraphrased a saying by Teddy Roosevelt that we had given to him when he graduated from high school: "That he was in the arena fighting and was not a timid soul."

Sue and I knew when we read the note that he was serious. We got in the car together, driving around town to try to find him. We must have driven around for hours before we went back home. Then, Sue's dad called her, very upset because the neighbor at the family's cottage called him and said Nick was there, asking if he had a key to the place. Sue explained to her dad that Nick was not well and might be trying to hurt himself. He had no idea about Nick's illness because we never told him or for that matter any of our family except my sister Marge and her husband. Although Nick had told my mom about the March incident, she begged him never to do that again, that the family loved him and would always be there for him.

Sue and I decided to drive up to the cottage to see if we could find Nick. The time changed from Eastern Standard to Daylight Savings. As it does every fall in the Midwest, the time change makes evening darkness come early. The fifty-mile drive in the dark on the country roads seemed endless. We were both exhausted from working most of the day, which made it hard to stay awake during the long lonely drive. About twenty miles from the cottage, we suddenly came upon several red flashing emergency lights from police cars on the road. There was an accident ahead. A white truck had flipped upside down in the ditch by the side of the road. The wheels were still spinning from the impact. A strong smell of burning rubber hung in the air from the locked brakes, which had caused tire skids along the pavement. Sue began to scream, thinking the accident might be Nick. Stopped by the police, we jumped out of the car to find out what happened. Although they wouldn't give us any details, we quickly learned the vehicle lying on its hood wasn't Nick's truck. Relieved but frightened and not knowing what we might discover if we found Nick, we got back in the car and continued our drive to the cottage.

The cottage was without heat and had been closed up for the winter. The cold, damp screened porch was empty. All the summer furniture was stored away. The only thing lying on the concrete floor of the porch was a long empty cardboard box.

I crossed the field next to the cottage and knocked on the neighbor's door. The neighbor was startled to see me. He acknowledged that Nick was there earlier, asking him if he had a key. When he told him he didn't, Nick left. Then he asked me a rather unusual question: "Do you have guns at the cottage?" Never in my wildest imagination did I think Nick had a gun. We never had guns at home, and we knew nothing about them. I had forgotten what Nick's friend told us about the conversation with the patient he met in the group therapy session. We were to learn that the empty cardboard box on the porch was from a shotgun Nick purchased on the way to the cottage. And the unusual question from the neighbor occurred because he had heard the cracking of gunshots in the nighttime air.

Apparently, Nick had taken some practice shots over the lake with the shotgun. Unable to find Nick at the cottage, we decided to return home.

Cell phones were new in the late '90s, and there weren't many cell towers, so reception was very poor. Although reception was spotty, we were able to receive a call from a friend of Nick's. He told us he had spoken to Nick and convinced him to call his counselor. His friend was able to arrange a three-way phone call with the counselor and us. The counselor confirmed he talked with Nick earlier in the evening. Nick had promised him to call us. Nick told his counselor he had taken too much of his medication. But he reassured us because he believed Nick would sleep it off somewhere. None of us knew that Nick had bought a gun.

We drove home and waited for Nick to call. Tim and Joe had already gone to bed. They had school the next day. After a few hours of waiting, Sue decided to go upstairs and lie down in Nick's bed while I fell asleep on the sofa in the living room. Shortly before 4:00 a.m., she came downstairs and said we needed a priest. She had fallen asleep in Nick's bed and had a dream of a tunnel with a bright light. In the dream, she was a bystander, watching a presence moving toward the light. When she awoke, she told me about the dream and that she believed the presence was Nick. I told her that I saw a bright light, too, while I slept for a few moments on the sofa. We called our parish emergency phone number, asking if our priest could come. We only lived a few minutes from the church. Father arrived quickly. And just moments after he arrived, the Sylvania police came to our door to tell us we needed to call the Michigan State Police in Ann Arbor.

I called them. A woman detective answered, asking me to identify myself. She said, "I am so sorry."

I knew immediately what she meant although I didn't want to believe what I heard. I told her "thank you" and hung up the phone. I looked at Father, the police officer, and Sue. She was already crying. She must have known by the look on my face what I was about to tell her. I just shook my head as I began to cry. They found Nick, and he was gone.

3

THE AFTERMATH

"Everyone can master a grief but he that has it."
(William Shakespeare, Saturday, November 15, 1997,
The Toledo Blade)

The week of October 27, 1997, was the worst of our lives. We lived by the verses in Psalm 46:1, "God is our refuge and strength, an ever-present help in trouble" (Holy Bible). Going to the funeral home, planning a funeral, choosing a casket for our twenty-year-old son, and selecting a burial plot—all were overwhelming. The question: How do we pick up the pieces when we were all shattered? Telling our family members and, most importantly, our other two sons that their oldest brother had died was the hardest thing we ever had to do.

The reality of what happened had not sunk in. We were in shock, running on autopilot knowing we had things to do. We thought somehow, by doing them, we could change everything and we would wake up realizing it was just a really awful dream.

My first call was to my dad and mom who still

lived in South Bend, Indiana. All Dad could say was, "Oh no!" After a brief silence, he told Mom, and I heard her screaming. Sue called her parents, Ed and Lois. Through her tears, she calmly asked them to help us notify her six sisters and three brothers.

Ed and Lois, who lived about twenty minutes away, immediately drove to our house. After wrapping their arms around us in comfort, they began the job of calling Sue's family. Her dad called Pat, her youngest brother. He didn't live too far away, and he arrived shortly after them. I remember him dressed in a crisp, white long-sleeve shirt with an open collar. His face was stoic as he agreed to drive up to Michigan to retrieve Nick's truck and personal effects.

Next, I called my sister Marge but first spoke to her husband Rick. I could hear him somberly telling her and then sounds of her crying loudly in the background. They notified my brother Dennis.

Morning began to break around 6:00 a.m. We had waited as long as we could before waking Tim and Joe. We woke them gently, telling them what happened during the night. They decided they wanted to go to school. We knew it would be the best thing to let them go so they could find comfort from their friends. Joe was extremely close to Nick. He kept saying, "I want to be where Nick is." The thought of this scared us, but we understood the pain he was experiencing. Tim, always quiet, holding his feelings inside, said very little. Being the second oldest, he and Nick were rivals. As the first-born, Nick was always paving the way for new things. Now, with him gone, Tim had to take on a new role and become the one to pave the way. It wasn't until a few weeks later that he broke down. I called St. Francis and spoke with Father O and Coach Cromwell, so they would be prepared when Tim and Joe came to school.

As the day wore on, my mom and dad drove in from South Bend about two-and-a-half hours away. Then a flood of family members, neighbors, and friends began to stop in or call as the news of Nick's death spread. The parents of Nick's senior classmate, who died just before school started, came to the house. They provided us so much support. They understood more than anyone what we were experiencing during those early hours and days after his death.

We never thought about how to arrange a funeral. We were in our forties. It was too early in our lives to be thinking about death. Both sets of grandparents and even my grandmother were still living. But we knew we had to begin making plans. Our parish priest was there with us throughout much of the day. We discussed having a funeral Mass at the parish church less than a mile from our home. We wanted the St. Francis's priests to preside over the service. They agreed to whatever we wanted. Father O would be the principal priest, but the Mass was celebrated jointly by several of the priests from the school. As time went on, we sat down together to choose the readings and music.

The funeral home and cemetery were also close to our home and church. We contacted the funeral home and arranged to meet with the funeral director the next day. The first task, once the coroner had completed an autopsy, was to bring Nick home from Michigan. As wild as it might seem, we felt we were bringing him back home. Maybe there was still hope he was alive. For Sue, it was hard to think of him alone in the funeral home at night. It was too difficult for us to think of him now as just a body. She still couldn't believe he was gone. I felt it was like being in a movie that I was watching. I was there, but it all seemed so unreal. We both felt hollow inside. We were in shock!

Sue was adamant about seeing him once he arrived in Sylvania. The funeral director told us he would need to determine if we could view him. He was concerned about the damage the gunshot may have done to his face. Sue continued to insist telling him she needed to know it was him. She told him what he looked like could not be worse than what she was imagining. She didn't care if it was just his hand or his foot. She needed to feel him and see him to be able to accept him as dead.

He died on a Monday, but we had to wait for the autopsy before he could be brought home from Michigan. The plans for his funeral were set for Saturday, the day after the St. Francis/St. John's football game. We knew kids from the two schools would want to be there because of Tim and Joe and because Nick was a well-known coach. A visitation was planned for Thursday evening and all day Friday. We closed the visitation around 5:00 p.m. Friday, allowing our sons and the other football players to get ready for the game. We knew Nick would have wanted it that way.

After meeting with the funeral director, we were

taken to a large room where several caskets of all different colors and price ranges were on display. We really didn't care about the cost. After all, we should have been spending money for his wedding, not his funeral.

We chose a beautiful brown mahogany casket. Its finish was smooth and sleek, showing the rich woodgrain of the mahogany. The inside was lined with a soft, off-white pillow, bedding, and a small bronze replica of the Pietà. Sue told me later the statue of Mary holding her dead son, Jesus, was symbolic to her. She said she now understood the pain and anguish felt by Jesus's mother or any mother who lost a son.

It wasn't until Nick was in the casket that we were allowed to see him. Thankfully, Nick's face had been spared. The wound from the gunshot took off the back of his skull. But his beautiful, thick, dark brown hair still covered much of his head, and every feature of his face was intact. Sue caressed his face. She still expected it to be warm. Instead, it was cold and hard. Beneath his leathery skin, as she touched his face, she could feel the popping of his facial bones shattered from the force of the gunshot.

Nick was so proud of volunteering as a coach for St. Francis. We had him dressed in his red coaching shirt, navy blue trousers, and coaching ball cap. His cap helped to hide the wound, but the funeral director said it was best not to keep the casket open very long. We decided the casket would be closed for his service. Only our immediate family and a very few close friends would have the opportunity to see him for one last good-bye. When the time came before the visitation, slowly, one-by-one, our family members filed past his casket. Some leaned over to kiss his face, others said good-bye, and some wept softly as they saw him lying there. Sue's mom said she didn't want to see him. She wanted always to think of him away at school. We respected her wishes.

Earlier in the week, we went to Toledo Memorial Cemetery to choose a plot where Nick would be laid to rest. It was the most gorgeous fall day. The sky was crystal blue with not one cloud present. The air was a little warmer for that time of year, but a gentle breeze was in the air. The trees in the cemetery were dressed in the height of their fall colors. Vibrant yellow, orange, and red leaves graced the many trees that dotted the cemetery grounds. The leaves just beginning to fall from the trees floated softly to the ground as the cemetery staff member led us to an area in the back of the grounds. It was right next to a pond where ducks and geese were lazily drifting along the blue-green water. Several other young people had been buried there. In fact, Nick's high school friend was buried just a couple of rows from the row where three plots were available. Sue and I wanted three plots together so that someday we could be laid next to Nick. Directly across the pond was a large granite monument with the name of the owners from the Italian Deli where Nick worked one summer. Immediately, we knew this as the place where we should bury our son. And we would come to visit it every day of the first year after his death.

During the week, Tim and Joe continued to go to

school. We didn't have to worry about how they were doing, as the St. Francis priests were watching over them. They would notify us about anything of concern. It helped us to know the guys were in good company at St. Francis. Later, they were able to participate in a grief support group for the students called The Silver Knights. We never asked them about it or how long they went to it.

Sue and I were able to sleep, but it was very difficult to eat. Friends and neighbors brought food every day, but neither of us had much of an appetite. We had to be reminded to drink fluids and take care of ourselves. It still seemed like a nightmare that we were living in rather than reality. We would get up each day and somehow get through another day.

Thursday, the visitation began at 5:00 p.m. and lasted until 9:00 p.m., and Friday it was from 10:00 a.m. until 5:00 p.m. Tim, Joe, Sue, and I stood greeting hundreds of people who came to visit. Lisa, Sue's sister, put together a video of Nick from our home movies. It began when he was little and continued up until he started college. The video played in a loop, continually running. There were photos of our family with Nick everywhere. Among them was a beautiful poem about Nick written by Sue's youngest sister Cindy. Several bouquets of fragrant flowers were on display, and more kept coming, deposited around the funeral parlor throughout the evening into the next day. Nick's mahogany casket with the lid closed sat at the front of the room. A small kneeler was placed in front of his casket for anyone who might want to plant their knees and say a prayer. I must admit that I became angry and pounded the top of the kneeler prior to the people's visit. I said to the Lord, "How could you let this happen?" The answer, once again was, "Do not lean on your own understanding," but I was still trying to do so. We concluded the Thursday evening visitation by saying the Rosary. I believe at this point our faith was shaken. God still held us together even after we were questioning His will to take Nick.

By the end of the day and a half, both Sue's and my legs were swollen from standing and speaking to all who came. So many people from our entire lives came to pay respects. Those from Nick's childhood, his grade school, high school, and college friends, as well as teachers from Ladyfield, St. Francis, John Carroll, and Bowling Green State University were there, and even friends from our own childhoods came or sent flowers, letters, and cards. The brothers of the fraternity from Bowling Green that Nick had recently pledged arrived. Each one handed Sue a red rose. Football players from St. Francis and St. John's, wearing their jerseys, came. Friends of family members, many whom Sue and I didn't know, attended. Jeane, Sue's older sister, told us the impact of Nick's death upon the community was further reaching than we would ever know.

Lisa helped Sue choose something to wear for the funeral. In the few days after Nick's death, Sue had lost at least fifteen pounds from the work of grieving. She had a simple black dress with a powder-blue silk top and an elegant black jacket in her closet that she hadn't been able to wear but now fit her. She felt the soft blue top of the dress was the same color as Nick's eyes. I really didn't care what I wore, but I remember it was my brown suit and my wingtip shoes. We still keep these things in our closet.

The morning of his memorial, we drove from our abode the short distance to the funeral home. We were given time for one last good-bye to our beloved Nick before the casket lid was forever closed. As a family, we placed special gifts inside the casket. Family members, who would join the procession of cars to the church, had gathered with us at the funeral home. Before Nick's coffin was put into the hearse, the funeral director gave some instructions, and a brief prayer was said. Sue and I along with Tim and Joe followed the hearse to church. Arriving there, we noticed the parking lot was packed with cars. Our church held about a thousand people. Every available seat was taken, with people standing in the side aisles. The upstairs choir loft was also overflowing with people. There wasn't room for anyone else.

Nick's coffin was taken from the hearse up the steps to the back of the church by pallbearers Tim and Joe, his cousin Chuck, and his friends Chad, Joel, Steve, and Adam. We followed up the steps into the rear of the church where the priest had us unfold a long white cover over the coffin. At that moment, it struck me. My God! Our son Nick is really dead. Everything I had tried to do to save him, I failed. I was defeated.

The priest with Holy Water consecrated the coffin before entering the church proper. Sue and I draped a special cloth over the casket and looked at each other with tears of sorrow. Slowly, we proceeded behind the coffin down the main aisle of the church. Each step felt like weights holding my legs from lifting my feet. Once again, an overwhelming feeling that I was watching a movie clouded my consciousness. Somehow, before I realized it, we were in the first pew on the church's left side, in front of the altar. The coffin with Nick's body was to our right in the middle of the main aisle between the pews and the altar.

Several priests from St. Francis were seated near the altar on the right side. As we had discussed, Father O was the lead priest, delivering the Mass with the assistance of the others who had once been Nick's teachers at St. Francis. The pallbearers were in the first pew to the right. My heart sank when I saw them, especially when I watched Tim and Joe standing there.

Family members, including Sue's aunt and Nick's confirmation sponsor, a Sister of Notre Dame, and some of our other relatives, gave the readings. Sue and I carefully chose the music for the Mass with the help of her aunt. To this day, both of us cry when we hear the songs at Mass. I gave the eulogy. I did what Nick asked me to do: read his letter quoting Teddy Roosevelt. I was numb as I read it and looked out to the crowd of tearing eyes. And Father O gave the most stirring homily, explaining how there were no answers as to why this happened except that Nick was ill and had now joined the "communion of saints."

When the funeral Mass was over, the coffin was wheeled down the center aisle leading the procession out of the church with Sue and me, our parents, and family members right behind it. Sue's dad guided her by the arm as we walked down the church's aisle. I looked about the solemn faces of the many people in the pews, and our entire lives flashed before me. I tried to keep from crying by politely smiling or giving a handshake as we walked past them to exit the church.

The coffin was loaded into the hearse. We got into the first car to make the short drive to the cemetery. The processions of cars from the church to the cemetery seemed endless. My friend from high school, who was a police officer, was able to block off the route from the church to the cemetery. A soft rain began to fall as we entered the grounds. It was as though even the angels were shedding tears of sadness.

The weeks that followed, Sue and I went with her parents to the retail store in Adrian, Michigan, where Nick bought the shotgun he used to take his life. We had absolutely no experience with guns, never having owned one, so we were surprised that Nick knew what to buy. We met the salesperson who sold Nick the gun. He couldn't have been much older than Nick. He told us that he explained to Nick what ammunition to buy and showed him how to load it. He showed us the form Nick completed to purchase the rifle. There on the form was Nick's signature. Then we met with the store manager. He said that he did not care that our son bought the gun there and committed suicide. Angry and incensed at his remarks, I walked away. Sue kept it together and said that was a very sad attitude. We walked out of the store together.

We also visited the site where Nick shot himself

and died, which was not far from the family cottage in Brooklyn, Michigan. It was all so unbearable. At the site where he died, we met the couple who found him. It was only a few miles from the cottage, just off a dirt road, with a gate that led to a beautiful meadow. Sue said it reminded her of the gate into heaven. I looked up into the sky and continued to ask our Lord, "Why?" The message back was there is suffering in this world and God gave His only begotten Son, Jesus Christ. That really made me wonder even more if this was a spiritual journey. On our search for him that bitter night, we just missed him…a fact that will haunt us forever.

4

COPING...

Picking up the pieces after Nick's death was the most difficult thing we have ever had to do in our lives. There really are no words to describe it. Our faith and each other helped us get through the pain as we took one step at a time each day. Sometimes we could only get through one hour or even just one minute at a time.

After Sue and I were off work for two weeks, we felt the need to get back to reality. We wanted to get things back to normal. Whatever normal meant. We still had two young sons to raise. We needed to keep our lives together, moving forward for them. We returned to work.

Tim and Joe continued to go to school and play football, which was a good thing. For Sue and me, it was scary to have to confront coworkers and friends. What we found were compassionate people who could not imagine the pain, and most told us that they were praying for us and even provided some literature on healing after such a tragic death.

I remember one time, shortly after coming back to work, one of my company's salespersons ran into me and said something like, "So sorry for your loss." I replied, "What are you referring to?' He looked at me dismayed and said, "the loss of your son." "Oh!" I again replied, "Thank you." For me, it was out of sight, out of mind. This same salesperson asked me if it felt like a defeat. I said, "Yes, it did." And we went on to talk about that. When I walked away and went into my office, I began to cry. That was among the first things that I felt: a terrible loss, a terrible defeat. I think Sue felt the same way. However, I was the dad. I am supposed to protect my family. I felt terrible guilt and pain. It was only by the grace of God that I worked through those feelings.

Sue continued as a corporate nurse, helping other people at her company. The good thing about her job was that she had an office where she could close the door and be alone if she needed. Working would take her mind off Nick for a little while, but then she would make the hour drive home, and the painful memories would be a flood on her mind. She told me later she shed many tears on her drives to and from work. She felt, as his mom, she was supposed to fix everything. But this was something she couldn't fix.

Together with Tim and Joe, we continued to have our family dinners. Afterwards, the guys would study or meet a friend while Sue and I would go to the park to walk and then later go to the cemetery. We had a bench with a plaque in his memory placed at the park where we walked.

We continued each day to get stronger at life. Tim was busy with his senior year of high school, getting ready to graduate. He was vying for the number one spot, not missing a beat. He graduated in 1998, only eight months after the loss of Nick. He ended up as the salutatorian, just one-hundredth of a point away from being valedictorian. How proud we were of Tim! It was yet another indication of the triumph over tragedy.

His graduation was an extremely emotional time for us, as well as for our family, when attending the ceremony. At graduation, he was serious and so poised. Tim gave a thought-provoking salutatorian speech to a large crowd of teachers, graduates, their parents, family members, and friends. It focused on the experiences in high school being part of the foundation of their lives. And how that foundation would endure throughout their lives. To explain his concept, he used an analogy of ripples created from throwing a stone in a pond. The ripples flow out from the center, but the center always remains. Like the ripples, the graduates were about to go out into the world. But what they experienced while at St. Francis would always be part of their center. In the end, Tim received a standing ovation. We could sense Nick's presence by the influence he had on his brother to succeed.

That summer, Tim began getting ready to go off to college at the University of Dayton, and Joe was preparing for an All-State football season. He was six-foot-four, gaining close to thirty-five pounds, a solid 290 pounds with no fat. The St. Francis team won the Toledo City Football Championship that year with a record of 10-1. Unfortunately, they missed the playoffs even though they were ranked seventh in the state of Ohio. That team was one of the best in St. Francis's history as well. Joe was named *The Toledo Blade* Player of the Year in Northwest Ohio, the only offensive lineman to be given such an award in its history. He also was voted first-team All-State; awarded district offensive lineman of the year; and received honorable-mention All-American honors.

Another sport Joe was involved in was track and field. He threw the shotput and discus. His sophomore, junior, and senior years, he took first place in the discus competition for the Toledo City League. He also placed in the shotput rankings those years. His junior year, he placed third in the state of Ohio at the Ohio State University. Ohio had some of the best discus throwers in the country. Sue and I cried at this feat. It was totally unexpected. Joe once again beat all odds. Between Tim and Joe, it seemed like triumph over tragedy was everywhere for our family. It was helping Sue and me and our sons heal.

Joe's senior year, the Ohio State track-and-field meet was held at the University of Dayton the same day as his high school graduation. He was our last son to attend St. Francis, and we really wanted him to go through his graduation ceremony. But he had other plans. He wanted to compete in the state meet, so we compromised. He walked the ceremonial walk down Bancroft Street from St. Francis High School to Gesu Church to attend the graduation Mass and then got up at the end of one of the speeches to get to the meet. Dayton is about three hours from Toledo, so all of us and one of his best friends, Kristy Gerber, took a private plane to Dayton so he could make the meet. He took fifth place in the state in discus, beating the St. Francis record by inches. That record, achieved by an athlete who went on to the University of Michigan and was an All-American football player, had lasted thirty-two years.

That first year we went to the cemetery every day unless I was traveling. We knew that Nick was not there, but we had to visit his grave to help us accept he was gone. At his grave, we left a notebook in a waterproof box with a pen. When we visited, we would write him notes or leave poems or cards. Intellectually, we knew he was not there, but emotionally it gave us peace to have a place to visit with him. Others who came to visit would leave him things, too. When he would have turned twenty-one, someone left him a bottle of beer. It was comforting for us to know he wasn't forgotten. As time went on, we visited less often and so did his friends. The first anniversary of his death, we held a ceremony at his grave, releasing two white doves into the sky, and one of Nick's friends sang "Turn! Turn! Turn!" by the Byrds. It was our way of releasing him once and for all.

They say that many marriages end up in divorce after such a tragedy. However, we continued to love and support each other. Although our grieving was simultaneous, it also was very personal. We needed time alone to reflect and pray after the tragedy of losing our son.

When I returned to work, I would go to a catholic church in Maumee, Ohio, and sit in the first pew in front of the Sacred Heart of Jesus. I asked the Lord again, "Why Nick? Why my family who were suffering so?" There were no answers, except the Lord was speaking to my soul, "Trust me." Shaking my head, I had nowhere to go except to the Lord. At the beginning, as I mentioned, I was angry at the Lord. He gave me peace, and I moved forward step by step. And I heard Him say, "Be still, my soul."

As for Sue, I believe she had similar feelings as mine. At first, she had a tremendous amount of anger. We had given Nick a desk when he moved into his apartment at Bowling Green, one of those that has to be assembled. She was good at doing things like that, so I let her put it together. After Nick died, we cleaned out his apartment, retrieving the desk. Sue decided she wanted to put it in his bedroom at home. His room was upstairs. Because the desk was large, it barely fit up the stairs. We struggled to get it up the steps, and Sue became upset. Crying, she took a hammer and repeatedly hit holes in it until it fell apart. She really was not mad at Nick or even that the desk did not fit; she was angry that he had died. We got the desk upstairs and in his room, and then she lay on the floor sobbing. She felt so awful that she put it back together and patched the holes. I understood. The desk stayed in his room until we moved.

We understand that we grieve differently. However, Sue and I were able to talk about it to each other. Looking back now, thankfully it is hard to remember the intensity of the pain from the grief. Every bone, every muscle in my body hurt. In one of the support groups we attended I remember someone saying, "The pain was as if someone threw her off a cliff." When you are going through it, there is no other explanation except for God's grace. I believe God was there to guide us.

Journaling has always been a way for me to express my feelings and my thoughts, so I gave Sue a journal to write down her thoughts, too. I thought it might help her. She wasn't able to begin writing in it until a few weeks after his death, and then she didn't write in it every day. But what she wrote she later shared with me. Here are some of her passages. They may help to explain the depth of our grief.

> November 18, 1997
> It's already over three weeks since Nick died but the reality of it all still escapes me. I think it is God's way of helping me heal. Then, suddenly it hits me, it is real, Nick is dead. I'll never hear his "hello Mom this is Nick" again. I'll never hug him when he squeezes me back. I'll never argue with him till I'm so angry I can't think. Then an overwhelming sadness strikes my heart and I cry till I am exhausted. This journey is exhausting. When will it end? How long does this road go? Please tell me it is a mistake. Nick is going to call and tell me it was all a joke. Please bear with me God. Help me walk this road alone.
> December 2, 1997

I've been busy writing notes to our many friends. It makes it difficult to write in this journal. I'm not very good at keeping a journal. I tried to keep one before when Nick was going off to college. I only wrote one entry, October 16, 1995. I had planned to show it to Nick one day when he was older. It was about how I was feeling as I know he was struggling. I never got to show it to him. I guess he knows now, doesn't he?

The days go by and we somehow get through them but not without many tears and emotions. I keep thinking I will see Nick soon. Then, I catch myself and realize it will be a long time before I see him again. I will never hold him again, or see his mischievous grin or smell his smell.

Why did this have to happen to us, to our Nick? Nicky, please know I love you. I will always love you. I will miss you everyday of my life, son.

Love,
your Mom

December 11, 1997
The thoughts of what happened never leave my mind. I think of Nick every waking moment. Even when life tries to creep into my thoughts, his death seems to prevail and I slip back into

thoughts of him. It still doesn't seem real. Where has Nick gone? When will I see him again? I need to pray to Jesus but sometimes I can't. Are my thoughts prayers enough?

How does this look from outside where I am? What must others be thinking of our journey? It is a very difficult journey. I am not as tired but just as sad.

March 4, 1998

Again, several weeks have passed since writing in this journal. Though time has passed, the pain continues. Oh but it has been such a short time since our loss of Nick. It is so ironic because although the time has been but a few months, the pain of remembering seems like he has been gone for a long time. I want to remember his voice but I have trouble hearing it. Because I only can hear it in my mind. I want to hold him but I can only hold him in my heart. Nick, why have you left us behind? Do you wonder yourself? My heart is so heavy it pulls upon my every step. I must labor to get through the days, the weeks, the months. My hope, my excitement, my joy in life has left. Each day is one more chore. I have learned to be patient, patient for the day when I will once again see his face and caress his head. My sweet, sweet son I love you. I miss you.

During 1998 and 1999, Sue and I continued to search for answers to Nick's death. We decided to attend grief counseling as a family. Sue had worked closely with the Employee Assistance Program in her job, so she was able to contact them for a recommendation. Our insurance paid for all of us to go. After a few meetings with the counselor, the guys and I decided we did not want to continue, but Sue kept going for a while. Eventually, she stopped going, too. It was too difficult to keep reliving the events of what happened. We had to learn to accept the new reality.

Sue and I kept thinking about the afterlife where we believed Nick was or is. We read every book we could find about life after death. Some of them were Christian books, and others were written by authors calling themselves mediums. I am not sure who the mediums really are or what they represent. Our faith and belief in God was stronger than ever. Our prayers were to let us one day be reunited with Nick.

Though frowned upon by the church, we even went to a medium. I did not think the medium was helpful, and I questioned why we went. I guess we were searching at every corner. We began attending different grief support groups. One was for survivors of suicide, another at our church for parents who lost children, and another that dealt with the spiritual realm for parents who lost children. We found it good to hear the stories of other people, especially parents dealing with the grief of losing a child no matter how the child died or how old the child was when she or he died. In the groups were people at all stages of their grief. Life as we knew it would never be the same, but it would get better with time as we learned to accept it as the new normal. We found it comforting to share with others who were dealing with one of life's greatest tragedies. It helped us realize that life could get better again and that one day we would laugh again. One thing that we all learned was that life does not stop for you.

We became active in the Suicide Prevention Action Network or SPAN, a national organization to promote suicide prevention through awareness and research. We also worked with the American Foundation for Suicide Prevention (AFSP), which later merged with SPAN. We helped AFSP to organize and participate in an Out of The Darkness Walk held in Bowling Green, Ohio, after the community was experiencing high-school kids dying of suicide. Walks similar to this are still being held all over the United States, helping to raise awareness about suicide and funding for research. As part of the event, an auction was held after the walk. For the auction, we were able to obtain a football autographed by Tony Dungy, head coach of the Indianapolis Colts. Coach Dungy's son James took his own life. Joe knew his son from his time with the Colts. In fact, we have a picture of Joe and James Dungy sitting next to each other on the sidelines when Joe was with the Colts. *Another reminder that no one is immune from suicide.*

Sue, as part of the wellness program for the company where she worked, did a testimonial of the walk, providing information on mental health and suicide on the company's intranet. She received comments from several employees, thanking her for helping to bring it out in the open.

To further the suicide awareness cause, Sue and I spoke to various groups in our community. At one of my daily visits to the church after Nick's death, a Sister of Notre Dame, a teacher at the school affiliated with the church, stopped me. She asked me why I came to the church every day on my lunch hour from work. I explained to her that I found comfort there after the death of our son. We talked a short time, and then she asked me if Sue and I could speak to the students who were getting ready for confirmation. She wanted them to hear our story about how our faith helped us through the tragedy.

We did speak to that group, and later Nick's sixth grade teacher, who was also a Sister of Notre Dame, contacted us. She was teaching at another catholic school in the area and wondered if we could speak to their confirmation class. We agreed and spoke again to a group of young people. Our message was that, in life, they will be faced with many difficult times where they may find their faith as the only thing to help them get through. We explained that it was our faith that helped us after the loss of our son.

Several of the students and their sponsors came up and introduced themselves to us after our talk. I remember a lovely young girl and her mother stopping to thank us for sharing our faith story. A deacon for the church also stopped to speak with us. He told us he was not really sure why we were asked to speak and did not see the connection. We just let it go. But three weeks later, we received a phone call from the church asking us to come to a funeral service. The lovely young girl died suddenly at home after a virus attacked her heart. Her father, a physician, was unable to revive her. Her friends and teachers were all in shock. At the funeral, the deacon apologized and told us he now understood the meaning of our talk.

Sue remembers a time when she worked on an inpatient oncology unit at the same hospital. The specialty of oncology was new to the hospital, and the unit was very small with a one-to-one ratio of nurse to patient. Occasionally, patients from the emergency room who had attempted suicide would be brought to the unit, when no other bed was available, for close observation and medical stabilization before being transferred to the psychiatric unit. The nurses working the unit would get upset because they could not accept that the patients trying to take their lives would be with cancer patients who were fighting for their lives. It was not until Nick died of suicide that she understood patients trying to take their lives were just as sick as patients with cancer. And they, too, were in a fight for their lives!

Later, Sue helped the social work department of the hospital she had worked for develop and hold a seminar on suicide for social workers and other health care professionals. She spoke, giving a personal account of a healthcare professional dealing with suicide. Sue even worked on a committee with the state of Ohio, setting up a program for suicide prevention.

We wanted to do something at St. Francis, so we established a scholarship in memory of Nick. To date, the scholarship has been awarded to twenty-three young men.

Nick, senior year in high school (1995)

Joe in Penn State uniform, senior year (2002)

Tim, Joe, and Sue, Big 10 Championship Game 2016

Tim in 2019

5

THE LIGHT BEGINS SHINING

"If God is for us, who is against us?"
(Holy Bible, Romans 8:31)

After finishing his high school football career, Joe was being recruited by Yale, West Virginia, and Illinois to play college football. He also was being recruited by Penn University for track to throw shot put and discus. He was a good student and had been accepted at several schools. He was accepted to Penn State College of Engineering, but they had not expressed an interest in him for football. Joe really wanted to play football at Penn State so we sent a tape of him to the Athletic Department. After several weeks, a grad assistant called to tell us he gave Joe's tape to Jay Paterno and he agreed to meet with us.

That January, Joe had an official visit at Penn University for track. Since Sue and Joe were making a trip to Pennsylvania, they decided to stop first at Penn State. I wasn't able to leave with them but joined them later in the weekend. When they arrived at Penn State, they learned there were official visits being held for the Penn State football recruits. Joe decided he was going to go to some of the recruiting meetings even though he wasn't invited for an official visit. Sue tried to convince him to wait for our meeting with Jay Paterno but he went into the meetings anyways. He sat through of few of the meetings and, by the time I got there, Joe had made up his mind he was not going to visit Penn. He was going to go to Penn State. Frustrated with Joe, Sue had to call the Track Coach at Penn and cancel his visit. Joe and I met briefly with Jay Paterno. Jay told us he had reviewed Joe's tape and was impressed with his potential. He told Joe he was going to share his tape with Coach Joe Paterno.

Weeks went by and we didn't hear anything. Then on February 11, 1999, what would have Nick's twenty-second birthday, we got a call from Jay Paterno offering Joe a preferred walk-on with no guarantees of him making the team. Joe was excited when we told him the news.

The summer of 1999, Tim was working for a company, sealing asphalt driveways and getting ready for his sophomore year in college. He excelled his first year at the University of Dayton. He had a good summer, dating young women and having fun with his friends, many from St. Francis. Tim did not give us any problems that we were aware of.

Joe was another matter. He was rebellious. He bleached his hair and pierced his eyebrow. It was interesting. He was working out hard, getting ready for Penn State football, but he was hanging out with friends who were just as wild as him. They too were mostly from St. Francis. We did everything we could to keep him out of trouble. We took away his car. I even followed him to parties to find out what was going on. He could not breathe without us knowing what he was up to.

That July, Joe was with us at the family cottage. Along with Sue and me were my brother, Den, and his wife. Joe was angry because he had to stay with us and not be with his friends. He began to argue with me. I lit into him. After all, I was his dad, who was trying to keep him on the straight and narrow. My brother looked at me in disbelief. Here was a giant guy, twice my size, and I was putting him in his place. That was the end of Joe's lip. But we couldn't wait to get him to Penn State and away from his friends.

In August, with summer coming to an end, we drove Joe to Penn State. We moved his things into his assigned dorm room where other football players were housed. After getting his room settled, we went with him to get measured for his helmet, cleats, and uniform. A swath of hair hung down across his forehead and into his eyes, but fortunately the pierced eyebrow stud was gone. As we were we leaving, he peered through his long blonde hair, looking at Sue and me, and said: "Don't worry, you will only have to pay for one semester. I am going to earn a scholarship." The seriousness in his voice made us believe he could do it, although we knew how difficult it would be because he was a walk-on. We let him know we were with him all the way. Sighing with relief, we left, thanking God that he made it to PSU.

We returned to our home in Sylvania outside of Toledo, where we had moved shortly after Nick's death, and went back to work. Sue was serving a petroleum company as their corporate nurse, and I was an HR executive at a company where I was also a shareholder. Life got back to normal, that is, until I was called into a special meeting with the company's operating committee. The CEO announced that the company was up for sale and they had a buyer. We were all speechless. I was thinking, *Oh no, now what?* I wasn't taken totally by surprise because I knew that someday this would happen. I began to have hope that the new company would be good. But the negotiations failed, and the potential buyer backed off. The families, the majority shareholders, were angry. It didn't take long, and a new buyer was found. But the sale of the company did not work out well for me because the new owners wanted a new team. Several of us, including me, ended up resigning. At least I received my stock, and my uncle Ted Iorio, a labor attorney, negotiated a very generous severance package.

Tim left for school. He served as a mentor to Joe that summer, which helped Joe to realize what he needed to do to get ready for Penn State. Tim came with us to some of the games. He needed a break from his intense studies. And Joe needed to see him as his brother and friend. It was only two years since we lost Nick. Both sets of Nick's grandparents, aunts, uncles, and cousins were following Joe and Penn State football. Penn State helped our family forget the pain of Nick's death for a while.

Joe called often to update us about his progress with the team. He had meetings with Coach Paterno and his staff. Of course, I was in awe. Joe couldn't understand and would ask me why was I in awe. All I could say was, "because he is Joe Paterno, a living legend."

On one of his many calls home, Joe told us he had moved up to third-team center and was playing guard. We didn't believe it. Penn State in pre-season was ranked as number two and number one by some national polls, and Joe was a true freshman walk-on. He dressed for the first game against Arizona, a team that was also highly ranked. It was the Pigskin Classic. Joe told us he might see some action in the game. We went to Beaver Stadium with an unbelievable feeling. This is really happening! When Joe came out onto the field, we cried. He had cut his hair. He was fit and trim in his uniform. Penn State beat Arizona handily. Although Joe did not see action in that game, he had transformed from a rebellious high school graduate to a serious young man.

A couple of games into the season, Joe got his first playing time against Akron. The University of Miami in Florida was next. The game was being played in the infamous Orange Bowl, and Miami was a ranked team. Joe called and told us he would be traveling with the team and would get playing time. We couldn't attend in person, so we organized a party in Toledo where we could watch the game on TV with St. Francis friends. The game started; Joe was playing guard. Our friends went nuts cheering for Joe. We could not believe it and never doubted Joe again.

Next was the Iowa game in Iowa City. And as we did with every game, Sue and I traveled. My parents, Jerry and Shirley Iorio, went with us to Iowa. We were so excited for every game, and Iowa was no exception. We woke my parents at the crack of dawn and drove to the stadium around 6:00 a.m. My mom later told me that she slept with one eye open so not to oversleep. Arriving at the stadium six hours before game time, Mom and Sue hung out while Dad and I walked around the Medical Center for the next three hours. By the time the game started, we were exhausted. When we finally settled into the stadium and sat down, Mom was doing a public relations job, bragging about Tim and Joe. Though still rated number two in the country, it was a close game. Our offense was not moving the ball. Joe came into the game in the third quarter playing center. He played like a senior. Holes opened up through the middle. Joe, number 63, was the talk of the stands. PSU won a hard-fought game over Iowa. I told my dad that the radio station interviewing Coach Paterno had asked him, "Who is Joe?" Coach Paterno said Joe Iorio is from Toledo, a walk-on, and an engineering student. Coach Paterno then said, "I have not even met his father yet." We were proud.

The next week, Joe called home. He said that he moved in as the starting center against Ohio State that Saturday. We could not believe it. *The Toledo Blade*, our hometown newspaper, had an article about it, and I was interviewed by a Toledo radio station. My message to the reporter was: although hard to believe that Joe made it to first string as a freshman walk-on, he was an outstanding athlete and smart. He knew all of the plays in a short time period.

Sue and I drove to State College on a Friday evening to attend the Ohio State game that Saturday. It was almost two years to the day of Nick's passing. It was such a distraction for us and the whole family. Walking around the campus before the game started, there was a radio station outside of Beaver Stadium (PSU). The reporter was asking in his microphone, "Who is this Joe Iorio?" As we walked by in disbelief, someone said, "Here are his parents." All we could say was that it had been truly an amazing time for our family.

The kickoff was around one hour away. Sue, our son Tim, and I had perfect seats in the stands at the fifty-yard line. ABC was televising the game to a national audience. Waiting for the game to start and watching the team warm up, we saw NFL hall of famer Lynn Swann walking up the steps. I was so excited to see him and said, over and over, I would love to talk with him. He kept walking closer to us in the stands. Before we knew it, he was standing in front of us, asking if we were the Iorios. Amazed that a football legend was asking for us, I was unable to utter a word. All I could think about was how he made an unbelievable catch in the Super Bowl with the Pittsburgh Steelers versus the Dallas Cowboys. Since I never seem to be without something to say, Tim chuckled and gave me a jab. Sue really didn't know who Lynn Swann was or what it meant for a football fan like me to meet him, so she was able to answer his questions without hesitation. He asked us, "Who is this Joe Iorio?" She said he was a freshman from Toledo, Ohio, who walked-on and was studying engineering. Before I knew it, she began to tell of his brother Nick's death as Joe's inspiration to play football at a Division I school. She went on to explain how Penn State helped raise us out of the valley from the loss of his brother. Lynn expressed his sympathy and concluded by saying Joe would be featured by ABC for this game.

Penn State beat Ohio State, gaining over 300 yards on the ground. Many times, the backs went up the middle over Joe or between Joe and the guards. The whole offensive line did a super job that day, another unbelievable time for the Iorios. There was a time when Joe was a senior in high school that Ohio State expressed interest in him but later dropped him. I am sure that helped fire him up. Plus, he dedicated the game in Nick's memory. We were to learn later that he dedicated every game in Nick's memory with NI 61 written on his wristband.

After the game, I finally met Coach Paterno. Tim and I met with Jay Paterno right outside the team's lockers. Jay introduced us to Coach Paterno. I said to Coach Paterno that my parents and brother lived in South Bend and were Notre Dame fans. But not anymore; they became Penn State fans.

The following week was a blitz of news media articles on the freshman walk-on. *USA Today* wrote a feature on Joe with a picture of him blocking an Ohio State player. I wasn't aware of the article until a vice president from my employer came over to my office and asked me if I saw the article about my son. It was concerning his rise to the starting position and the Nick Iorio story. The reporter interviewed Tim regarding the fire that was lit in Joe because of Nick. Sue talked about how this went from being the Nick story to the Joe Iorio story. Articles also appeared in *The Toledo Blade*, several newspapers in Pennsylvania, and the *New York Times*.

The next game was at Purdue with Drew Brees as the quarterback. Purdue was ranked while Penn State was number two in the country. All-Americans Courtney Brown, LaVar Arrington (numbers one and two, respectively, in the 2000 NFL draft), Brandon Short (drafted in the fourth round), and David Macklin (drafted in the third round) were part of this dynamic team. The game was nationally televised by ABC. Penn State won the nail-biter game with Joe starting at center. Sue and I, along with Tim and my nephew Tony Iorio, and my dad, Jerry, attended the game. Watching Joe, dressed in his suit and getting off the team bus, I remember thinking it was hard to believe all this was happening. At the beginning of the game, ABC, with Lynn Swann, Bob Griese, and Brad Nessler reporting, some of the best college football commentators ever, was doing a highlight on Joe before an upcoming play. Sue and I did not know about it because we thought Gary Danielson and Brent Musburger talked about Joe during the Ohio State game. We taped every game so we could watch them when we got home. We watched the tape of the game in disbelief. Lynn told the Nick and Joe story to Bob and Brad. Lynn concluded by saying that, in talking to their parents Sue and Tim, they felt Nick's spirit was with Joe. Brad went on to say that the parents have been in the valley but are now rising out of it through Joe and Penn State football. We couldn't believe they told our story on national TV. When we heard it, we cried. That is when we thought triumph was overcoming the tragedy.

Tim was in the midst of transferring from the University of Dayton to Penn State. He fell in love with the campus and found himself closer to Joe. Sue and I kidded that they were like twins together, born only eighteen months apart. As a family, we began slowly moving forward, step by step. But we still had some very difficult moments of grief. Attending grief counseling sessions and attending support groups with other parents helped us learn how to handle our grief.

The year 2000 was an up-and-down year. After resigning from my job when the company I loved was sold, it was time to move forward. I began a job search while doing consulting work. Sue continued working at the petroleum company but was very nervous about my split from the company. It was a stress that we didn't need. Finally, after a year, I received an offer from a farm supply company in Northwest Ohio. My new job was as Human Resources/Labor Relations Leader. The company was struggling, and, while a turnaround almost occurred, they filed for bankruptcy during the 2001 recession. I worked on an outplacement program to help folks who were losing their jobs find new employment. My job only lasted seven months.

Tim was a junior at Penn State. He was happier than we had seen him for a while. He was an outstanding student in a pre-med curriculum. His goal was to go to medical school and become a doctor. Like Joe, he was determined to succeed. It was such a blessing to watch our sons grow and develop after losing their older brother. There was no doubt Nick was an inspiration in all our lives.

The spring of 2000, Joe received the Italian American Athlete of the Year award from the Toledo chapter as a freshman. It was indeed an honor. Coach Paterno was the keynote speaker and recognized Joe as an amazing young man. Many of our friends and family members were there to participate in such a proud moment. It was another example of where triumph was present over tragedy.

While the Italian American Athlete award was a highlight, the adversity Joe faced later in the summer demonstrated how quickly things can turn. During the 2000 summer training camp, Joe came down with mononucleosis. He was living in an apartment with all-senior football players. They were busy and would come and go. Being Joe's first summer away from home, it was difficult for us to know he was sick. We drove to State College to visit him and were astounded. He had lost twenty-five pounds and looked terrible. The mono made him very fatigued; all he wanted to do was sleep. He wasn't allowed to come home, so we stayed awhile and tried to nurse him back to health. We washed his clothes, changed his bed linens, cleaned his apartment, bought him groceries, and cooked him meals.

Joe was contemplating leaving the team because of the illness. We wondered if he would be given a redshirt. We met with Joe's offensive line coach, Dick Anderson, who scheduled a meeting with Coach Paterno the next day. Sue, Joe, and I were there. I was in awe because of his huge office with iconic pictures of all the past Penn State greats like Franco Harris and Heisman Trophy winner John Cappelletti. Sue was not that impressed. When we arrived, Joe had his cap on. Coach Paterno asked him to take it off, which he promptly did. We all sat around a table and, one-by-one, spoke of our concerns. It was Sue's time to speak, but Coach Paterno kept interrupting her. Finally, she spoke up and politely said she was not finished talking. Surprised at her response, Coach Paterno said, "Now I know where Joe gets his toughness."

He told Joe that if he wanted to leave the team, okay, but he did not want him to quit school and would work on getting Joe an academic scholarship. Joe had proven he was an outstanding student, getting good grades while juggling football and his studies. In fact, some of the players said he always had his nose in a book while waiting for football meetings. That was Joe's significant moment; he realized that Coach Paterno was not just about football. Sue and I had a renewed respect for Coach Paterno. Joe decided not to quit the team. We were thankful to God for helping Joe and the family see this adversity through.

Joe did not redshirt that year because the team needed him desperately to anchor the line. With Joe playing center and the team coming together, Penn State won their last five out of seven games, crushing a good Michigan State team on the final senior game day.

Joe's junior year, the tragedy of 9/11 occurred. Penn State was supposed to play at Virginia the following day. We had driven to Virginia with my parents and were staying at a resort near the university, about ninety miles away from the Pentagon. That morning, we were watching the television news when the pictures of two planes crashing into the Twin Towers in New York City came on. Sue and I both shouted that it was no accident, war was upon the United States.

There was a conference for insurance companies being held at the resort. Many of the people staying there were from New York and New Jersey. The place emptied, as people were anxious to return home. All we wanted to do was get to Penn State as quickly as possible to be with our boys. We drove to Penn State. On the drive back, the cars and trucks went slowly and showed a courteous disposition that I had never seen before on the road. There was a lot of sadness on the faces of the drivers.

The 2001 season started out with an 0-4 record. Then came a huge win over twentieth-ranked Northwestern in the game's last few seconds. Penn State finished the disappointing season at 5-6, but then came Joe's senior year, 2002.

6

AN AMAZING TIME

"And then we learn that the storms of life have driven us not upon the rocks but into the desired haven."
(George MacDonald, *Vision 2000*, S.J. Mark Link, Tabor Publishing, 1992)

Tim graduated from college in the spring of 2002 and was accepted to the Ohio State Medical School to start in the fall. I was doing a lot of consulting. Sue was steady with her job. Joe was working out hard in the off-season. It was a very blessed time for our family.

My parents, Sue's mom, Sue, and I attended the White Coat Ceremony for Tim at Ohio State. The ceremony welcomes the incoming first-year medical students. It was such an emotional time for all of us. Questions lingered: Why could Nick not be with us to celebrate this and his own accomplishments? As Proverbs states, "Do not lean on your own understanding," a verse that carries all of us, even today.

Joe's senior year, the Penn State football season began with a win over Central Florida University at Beaver Stadium. Penn State played Nebraska in the second game. Nebraska was ranked seventh and Penn State twenty-fifth. In front of more than 110,000 persons, Penn State won the game by a convincing 40-7 score. As the sports commentators said, "Penn State is back." After two lean seasons, Happy Valley was back on top and very happy.

The overall season was a huge success with nine wins and three losses and a ranking of tenth in the nation. Two of those losses were in overtime against ranked teams, Iowa and Michigan. The third was to Ohio State by a score of 13-7. Ohio State eventually went on to be the National Champions that year. Larry Johnson gained over 2,000 yards, and the offensive line, anchored by Joe, was considered the best in the Big Ten conference and one of the best in the nation. The line and the team had come a long way.

The football banquet held in December was extremely emotional for our family. Joe made Academic All-American, graduating in four years while playing football, an unbelievable feat for a walk-on. My parents, along with Tim, attended the banquet and ceremony in the Penn State basketball arena. Before the banquet, Coach Paterno took pictures with our family, which to this day are still proudly displayed in our home.

During the banquet, we sat with Robbie Gould and his family. Robbie was to become one of the best field-goal kickers in the NFL. When it was Joe's time to come forward, Sue and I walked arm-in-arm with him down the aisle toward Coach Paterno. Tears streamed down our faces. It was five years since we lost Nick and then this journey with Joe. Tim was a big part of it, too, serving as Joe's mentor. As we approached Coach Paterno, tears gleamed in his eyes. We all hugged each other for we knew, except for one more game, that this was the end of our Penn State football journey. Our feelings toward Coach Paterno have always been and will continue to be those of gratitude. He was a wonderful person. He gave our son Joe a chance and helped all of us to overcome the worst defeat of our lives. Coach Paterno was quoted in a news conference saying, "Joe Iorio has done a very good job." Paterno, the reporters went on to write, regretted that he had to play him as a freshman. "Iorio is a solid student playing an important position. He and his family are remarkable people, and he will be tough to replace."

The last game was on New Year's Day 2003 with Penn State versus Auburn, the Capital One Bowl in Orlando, Florida. It was a disappointing loss, 13-9. Joe received a lot of kudos from the ABC announcers about his chances of playing in the NFL. After the game, Coach Paterno had a get-together with the seniors and their parents. It was a down-to-earth event, the Penn State way. I personally met former Penn State and NFL greats Ki-Jana Carter and Kyle Brady. Earlier in the week, I met another great, Franco Harris. It was hard to believe, though, that Joe's career was done at Penn State. But a new beginning was now emerging.

With all the excitement of Penn State football, Tim was working hard his first year of medical school at Ohio State. There was no fanfare, but the family knew what Tim had accomplished to get to that point. It was very stressful for Tim, and Joe's football career had been a stress reliever. As proud as Sue and I were of Joe, we were just as proud of Tim. Unless one has a child going to medical school, it is impossible to understand the challenges. I even heard Coach Tony Dungy of the Colts, when speaking about his sister who is a surgeon, say, "Being a doctor is much tougher than trying to punch a touchdown on fourth and goal." (Comments made at the Fellowship of Christian Athletes' Dinner, Toledo, Ohio, 2004.)

I was doing human-resources consulting work for a major construction association located in the Washington, DC, area. It was rewarding work, but it was coming to an end. I was torn between finding a full-time job or working to build the consulting business. Sue was still nervous about the future. Again, Penn State football was a saving grace during another stressful time. Sue was steady in her work, which became so important during my transition period. It was five years now since we lost Nick. Although we moved forward and received many blessings from God, it was still a never-ending heartbreak. Somehow we were receiving the strength from God promised in Psalm 46:1: "just turn to Him for refuge and strength." This holds true today for our family.

In February 2003, Joe was selected to play in the Hula Bowl game in Maui. We were so grateful that he received such an honor to represent Penn State along with outstanding players from across the country. The Pro Bowl was the next day in Hawaii, and NFL scouts were everywhere. But the game was quickly put into perspective when, on February 1, 2003, the space shuttle Columbia exploded, killing all seven of the crew members. The game was played a couple of days later, dedicated in their memory as the entire nation mourned. Joe's team came back in dramatic fashion and won the game. Sue and I met Joe's agent. He said that several teams were interested in Joe, including the Pittsburgh Steelers and Super Bowl champions Tampa Bay Buccaneers. It was an amazing time. We also met some very wonderful coaches that day: head coaches from Minnesota, Marshall, and national champions 2001, Miami.

Penn State held workouts before the April football draft. Many of the teams came to see All-American players like Larry Johnson, Michael Haynes, Jimmy Kennedy, and Bryant Johnson. The headlines from *The Patriot-News* by Bob Flounders (April 21, 2003) read, "Don't count PSU's Iorio out in upcoming draft." Why? Joe had outstanding workouts in all phases. Afterwards, the Steelers and Buccaneers confirmed that they wanted Joe to attend personal workouts. Joe was not invited to the NFL combine, which makes us wonder even today. Joe should have been at the combine; he was the best offensive lineman on Penn State's team, according to many sportswriters. But he was used to being the underdog and rose to the occasion. His workouts went extremely well, especially with the Steelers.

NFL Draft day came in April. My dad, Sue, Tim, my brother, and I were at Penn State during draft time.

Joe, my brother, and I went golfing to calm down the nerves. We all knew he would not be drafted on the first day. We thought that he would on the second and final day in the fourth to seventh rounds. Many newspapers had interviewed Joe about this. Joe also said that he could go as a free agent. The Steelers indicated to him that they were interested in drafting him in the sixth or seventh round. Joe understood the NFL game, as he told sports reporter Ron Musselman of *The Toledo Blade* in an April article, that one never really knew what would happen.

The second and final day of the draft, Joe's name wasn't called. We were all very upset, except for Joe. I stormed outside his apartment and began thinking to myself, *How could this be?* Then immediately after the last player was drafted, Joe received a call from the Colts's head coach Tony Dungy.

As Rick Gosselin wrote for Texas Cable News (May 19, 2003), "Even players not drafted can rise and shine in [the] NFL." He complimented Joe for being an Academic All-American and the first walk-on as a freshman to start for Joe Paterno. Some wonderful accolades came through for Joe. Besides receiving the Verizon Academic All-American award, he was awarded a postgraduate scholarship. He was only the eleventh Penn State football player in the history of the school to receive both awards (gopsusports.com/pressrelease, July 1, 2003).

Joe received a lot of publicity concerning his career at Penn State and the draft. He beat the odds from a walk-on to the NFL. It was another example of triumph over tragedy. We are certain that Nick's spirit and influence had something to do with it through the grace of God and Jesus.

Tim continued to work hard in his second year of medical school, and then more adversity struck our family. My dad, Jerry, became seriously ill. Tim was able to get a nationally acclaimed doctor at Ohio State's Medical Center to see Dad. He was diagnosed with a horrible lung disorder, pulmonary fibrosis. We were in a state of shock. Dad did tell me while we were walking along the beach in Orlando that he was having a hard time breathing and was worried. So were all of us, especially my mom, Shirley. While Dad was fighting the disease, Joe's NFL career with the Colts became another big distraction for my dad and our family. During all of this, I was still doing lean-manufacturing consulting for a table-pad company in Lagrange, Indiana. The president of the company contracted important work to me. Sue was doing fine with her work at the petroleum company.

Summer of 2003 was a paradox for our family. On one hand was my dad, sick and fighting for his life, while on the other, the joy of Joe going to the Colts with the respected and admired Coach Tony Dungy. Dad had surgery at Ohio State, and it was confirmed that he had pulmonary fibrosis. His spirits were still high as he focused on Joe and the Colts.

Joe entered the Colts camp in July as another journey began for him. He was nervous and excited to show that many of the NFL scouts were wrong. He had Nick Iorio looking over his shoulders; we are certain of that. Joe began as a backup center to future hall of famer Jeff Saturday. And Joe was playing with the great quarterback Peyton Manning. We just could not believe all of this was happening. Joe showed the world that he beat the odds again.

7

THE NFL AND BEYOND

"He wants me."
(Joe Iorio, regarding his Draft Day phone call from Coach Tony Dungy, April 2003)

Joe was busy trying to make the Colts roster. The NFL is not for the weak at heart. Tim, who was entering his second year of medical school at Ohio State, continued to serve as a mentor to Joe. Medical school is as challenging as it gets, and Tim was meeting the challenge head on. We were so proud of both Tim and Joe. Sue continued to be there for Tim and Joe. I was enjoying consulting work for a business in Ohio and Indiana in the practice of lean manufacturing. I also was there for our two sons, always reminded about what they went through in high school after the loss of their brother Nick.

Joe lived in Indianapolis, and he would get lonely. We thought a puppy might give him company, so as a gift we bought him a beautiful female boxer. He was thrilled and named her Bishop. Sue and I helped take care of her at the beginning while Joe was in the Colts's camp. Later, Bishop went with him when he made the Colts's roster. She traveled around the country with Joe. After he left the NFL, she was always with him until one dark day in 2014 when we lost her to a blood disorder. We loved her so much!

At the end of the Colts's camp, Joe made all of the cuts to stay with the team—an amazing feat for a rookie free agent. There was one more cut to go to make the fifty-three-man roster. Sue and I went to be with Joe in Indy to find out if he made the cut. He did not call us, so we were worried that he did not make it in spite of an excellent preseason according to Coach Dungy. We got to his apartment, and he walked out. We knew immediately that he did not make it. We felt devastated for him. But little did we know that it was not over for Joe. We were all learning what the NFL was about, especially for a player not drafted. Tim talked with Joe and as always encouraged him to hang in there.

After Joe was cut from the Colts, he received calls for workouts with Minnesota and New England. That is how the NFL works. It is never over until it is over. I felt Joe was demoralized by the Colts's cut. Nothing came of the workouts with Minnesota or New England; however, Miami called him and immediately placed him on their practice squad. Joe did not like Miami. I flew to Miami to support him with the change. Together, we sat in a hotel room with the A/C cranked down to 65 degrees because Joe wanted it cold. I sat there freezing and remember watching *Lord of the Rings*. I took a walk alone along the beach. Joe did not want to come. I really thought this was it; he was going to quit. Miami later cut him; his heart was not in it. When we were driving to the airport, believe it or not, the Colts called him back to the practice squad. All of a sudden, he was smiling again. Wow, another rollercoaster ride was upon us.

Dad's illness was getting worse. He was really struggling to breathe. Mom was beside herself because of his constant coughing with every breath. He began to lose weight. It was hard to watch him lose the battle with the pulmonary fibrosis.

But Tim was doing well in medical school, and Joe was back with the Colts. It was all so overwhelming as we moved forward from the loss of Nick. Sue and I continued to pray to the Lord, read scripture, and attend church. Without our faith, I do not think we would have been able to support my dad and our two sons.

Joe finally made the roster of the Colts. It was almost unbelievable. He dressed for a couple of games, but just as soon as he would be signed to the roster, they would cut him. He became a hot commodity and even had calls from Cincinnati and Seattle. He stayed with the Colts on and off for almost two years. While Joe was with them, they made it to the NFL Division Championship versus the Patriots twice, losing both times. The second time, Joe sat next to Peyton Manning on the plane ride back to Indianapolis. Joe was impatient. He wanted to start, not just play backup center to Jeff Saturday.

Finally, in 2005, after being cut from the Colts's

practice squad only to be called again for camp, he decided he'd had enough with the Colts. Instead, he signed with the Pittsburgh Steelers for their camp. Russ Grimm, a future hall of famer from time with the Washington Redskins and a member of the team's infamous hard-nosed hogs, had contacted Joe.

On July 14, 2005, Dad, or Pa as we called him, died. It was another dark time. Pa believed in the Lord, and, by his faith and the grace of our Lord, he went to be at home. Early that morning, Mom, my sister, brother, and I received a call from the hospital in South Bend, Indiana, that we better come quickly. When we got there, Pa was unresponsive in a coma. As we all gathered around his bedside, Pa suddenly sat up, raising his arms, reaching out his hands as if to heaven, then fell back and died. A priest who was with us said he believed that Pa saw his loved ones. I believe that Nick, his mom and dad, and other loved ones were there to greet him.

Sue, Tim, and Joe came to South Bend to pay their respects. Eventually, we brought Pa's ashes back to Toledo where a Mass celebrating his life was held at Christ the King Church. Unbelievably, Father Brown, the priest who married Sue and me in 1975, and Father O, the priest from St. Francis who presided over Nick's funeral, said Pa's Mass. We believe these were more than coincidences, just like in 2002 when my Grandma Kaintz died. She was very important in our life. I was living with her and my Grandpa Kaintz when I met Sue. She would help babysit when our kids were young. She was especially close to Nick, watching him as a toddler while we both worked. Her death occurred on July 25, Sue's and my wedding anniversary.

Pa's ashes were buried close by Nick's grave in Toledo Memorial Cemetery, something Sue arranged at Pa's request shortly before his death. When he learned that Sue was able to find a plot close to Nick, he felt he could die in peace.

Tim went back to Ohio State where he would begin his summer studies in medical school. I returned to my job that I began in 2004 as a Human Resources/Labor Relations Leader for an automotive company in Northwest Ohio. The firm had big labor issues, so I was busy. Sue was happy that I had found a good job. Joe was off to report to the Steelers camp in Latrobe, Pennsylvania. When we visited Joe one week, he got us a pass for the field during the Steelers camp. Overlooking the field, we noticed a church. We thought of it as a good sign.

The camp was brutal. The Steelers had double sessions in full pads, a practice that was later banned by the NFL. As exciting as it was, we were nervous because all the players were big, powerful, and fast. We never imagined how physically and mentally tough a player had to be to make it in the NFL. But Joe was hanging right in there. Standing there on the field watching Joe, someone said, "You must be so proud of him." I was proud, but I was also very anxious for him. There we were next to Coach Bill Cowher, the Bus (Jerome Bettis), Jeff Hartings (All-American from Penn

State), and Max Starks (a six-foot-eight, 350-pound giant offensive tackle).

Later that weekend, the Steelers had a preseason game at Heinz Field against the Philadelphia Eagles. Joe got to play at center throughout that game, and he played well. Following the game, Coach Cowher said in a radio interview that Joe Iorio played very well and had much potential.

Joe started at fourth team. He was moved up to third team and was just a short distance from second team. Joe hated camp and starting out at fourth team. When he had time off from camp, he would drive to Cleveland to visit family and take a break. Sue's brother, Dr. Edward Floyd, and his family lived in Cleveland. Ed was an All-American wrestler and football player at John Carroll University. He was instrumental in mentoring Joe that summer. Because of Ed, Joe was able to endure the Steelers camp.

Shortly after the Eagles game, Joe got injured during preseason. The trainer thought he had a groin strain, often called a groin pull. He came home for a break and was complaining about the pain in his groin even though he wasn't working out. Simple movements like coughing and sneezing caused pain. It goes without saying, there was no way he was able to play without experiencing significant pain. It seemed like more than just a groin pull. We eventually found out that what was thought to be a groin pull turned out to be a sports hernia. A sports hernia is actually a tear in the structure of the groin, and, while it may get better after several weeks of rest, the best treatment is surgical repair. It is difficult to diagnose, requiring a skilled practitioner.

Joe was on the way back to the Steelers camp after the break when he got a call from a team official telling him that he was cut. The official told Joe to turn in his playbook. A very cold and heartless act by the Steelers, but that is the NFL. Without a job, Joe had no medical insurance. We tried to get a medical insurance policy for him, but even if we could, this was considered a preexisting condition and likely work-related, which wouldn't be covered.

He told his agent that he wasn't able to do anything without pain. Under the players' contract, Joe had fifteen days to determine what was going on medically and to file a grievance against the team. According to the contract, a player who is injured while playing is supposed to be placed on Injured Reserve (IR) instead of being cut. So it appeared he had grounds for a grievance. But it was up to him to get the correct diagnosis. Since the sports hernia is difficult to diagnose, Joe had to get at least two independent medical evaluations to confirm the diagnosis. He went to three independent surgeons in three different cities, and it was determined he had a tear and needed surgery. His agent, an attorney from Philadelphia, immediately filed a grievance against the Steelers, but they denied him workers' compensation.

We decided it was best for him to have surgery as close to home as possible so he could recuperate nearby. His third evaluation was performed by a wonderful female surgeon at the University of Cincinnati

Medical Center. She was very familiar with athletes, having worked with the Cincinnati Reds. Joe decided he wanted her to perform the surgery. I drove Joe to Cincinnati Medical Center where he underwent an outpatient procedure. After surgery, we drove back to our home in Sylvania. It was a three-hour drive. Looking back, we should have stayed overnight in Cincinnati. Joe was in agony during the long drive home. I had to stop several times to give him a break. I felt so bad and was so angry at the Steelers. Believe it or not, the day after he had surgery, the Cincinnati Bengals called and wanted to sign him. They had no idea what was going on or that he had been injured.

Joe was able to settle the grievance prior to the decision by the arbitrator. The players' union attorney really wasn't that interested in representing Joe's interest, so we retained our own attorney to represent him, Ted Iorio. Uncle Ted negotiated an excellent separation package, which included a pension for his time in the NFL. The union attorney said that he had never seen this benefit before in his twenty-five years for a player who was on the bubble like Joe.

Joe's football career was pretty much over in 2006 at age twenty-five. He did have brief tryouts with the Chiefs and NFL Europe. Little did we know at the time that NFL Europe was about to go bankrupt, and it did not work out. Joe was fed up with the NFL. It was time for him to give up football and move forward. He decided he was done. While Joe received a scholarship to continue his education, he decided not to return to school and began a career in marketing/sales of medical devices. It took him several months to figure out what he wanted to do with his life, but once he did he became very successful.

Tim graduated from medical school and went on to complete a five-year residency in orthopedics at Henry Ford Hospital in Detroit from 2006 to 2011. Henry Ford got him ready for his orthopedic surgery/hand surgery fellowship at Thomas Jefferson in Philadelphia, one of the leading programs in the country. Tim studied under some of the best doctors in the United States, graduates from schools like Harvard and Yale.

Tim also became engaged to a beautiful woman, Tara Thornton of Oakwood, Ohio. They later married in 2008, and in 2010 our first grandchild, Tad Nicolas (named after Nick), was born in Royal Oak, Michigan. It was a very busy time for Tim and Tara as they put their house up for sale and moved to Philadelphia for his fellowship. With a new baby and not making a lot of money as a resident, they never complained. Ironically, many of his friends were in business making good money. Sue and I kept reminding him that it would all work out and one day he would be glad he became a doctor.

Then on December 1, 2011, baby Reese was born in Philadelphia, another miracle from God. Sue and I flew to Philly for Christmas to see our little princess and two-year-old Tad. In my thoughts, the circle of life became reality. I often thought, *Now, we have two grandchildren, helping us through another year and Christmas without Nick.* A couple of years later, Tim and Tara blessed us with our third grandchild, Beckett. That same year, both Sue's mom and my mom died. We had so much joy and yet so much heartache.

Following Reese's birth, we returned to Westerville, Ohio, where we were living after selling our home in Sylvania. I was getting ready to teach as an adjunct professor at Otterbein University in Westerville. I was able to fulfill a lifetime dream to go back to school for a PhD at Indiana Tech and teach at the collegiate level after a successful career in business. (I also graduated from the University of Toledo with a Bachelor of Arts degree and, as noted earlier, with a Master of Arts degree from the University of Illinois.)

Sue was driving over an hour to her job. She went on to become a nurse practitioner, graduating from Kent State University, and eventually retired from the petroleum company in 2014. Sue also had a Master's degree from the University of Michigan (with a nursing diploma from St. Vincent's in Toledo and a Bachelor of Science degree from the University of Toledo).

We have always wondered why this disease called mental illness struck our family. Because it is so complex and still misunderstood, it is hard to accept. After losing Nick, I remember saying to Nick's doctor, "I never knew you could die from it." But we know we are not alone.

8

MENTAL HEALTH & GUN SAFETY

> We need commonsense gun safety.
> (Paraphrase, Governor John Kasich, Ohio:
> John Kasich's 2016 Presidential Campaign Speech on
> Gun Control)

This book has been written about our family's tragedy of losing our son Nick to suicide in 1997 and how we survived the heartbreak. Our goal is to help people who have lost a child, or anyone for that matter, to suicide. It is about the grief we experienced with Nick's suicide and how we were able to move forward to live our lives. We could not finish this book without discussing the relationship of mental health and gun safety because Nick was able to purchase a gun and take his own life while being treated for a mental health disorder.

We need to start with a research definition of mental health. The National Institute of Mental Health (NIMH) defines mental health as "a mental, behavioral, or emotional disorder." The statistics of any mental illness are startling. NIMH reported that in 2017 there were an estimated 46.6 million adults aged 18 or older in the United States with any mental illness (AMI); this number represented 18.9% of all adults, with AMI higher among women than among men. Young adults aged eighteen to twenty-five years had the highest prevalence of AMI. All races have been affected by AMI (Caucasian, African American, American Indian/ Alaska Native, and Asian).

There are many medications for treatment of the mental health disorders of anxiety and depression. Bipolar disorder can include symptoms of depression and anxiety. Antidepressant medications, called SSRIs, are often used in combination with other medications for treatment of bipolar disorder. Prozac was the first SSRI medication approved by the FDA in 1987, just ten years before Nick began taking it. As more research has been conducted since then, the use of Prozac and other SSRIs with children and adolescents between the ages of eighteen to twenty-four has become controversial, according to Mayo Clinic (www.mayoclinic.org). The Food and Drug Administration warned in 2004 that Prozac may be harmful to this age group, causing the potential of suicidal thoughts and suicide. As a result, the FDA mandated that black-box warning labels concerning this possible side effect be put on Prozac and other SSRI medications.

In 1997, when we met with the detective investigating Nick's death, he asked us if Nick was on any medication. He told us he found that more persons, especially adolescents, who had committed suicide were taking Prozac. Since Nick's death, research has come a long way in helping to understand the effects of antidepressants. Parents must be aware of these potential dangers and continue to ask the questions.

Suicide is the taking of one's life (*Harvard Public Health*, Spring 2013, p. 3). The Harvard study reported that more people kill themselves with a firearm each year than are murdered with one. In 2010 in the United States, 19,392 people committed suicide with guns, compared with 11,078 who were killed by others (*Harvard Public Health*, 2018, p. 3). It is a major societal problem in the United States. According to the Harvard study, most Americans agree. Even the National Rifle Association (NRA) agrees with this. The NRA philosophy will be reviewed below.

We have read countless articles concerning the pros and cons of gun safety (some might term it as gun control). We were asked to serve on a panel on gun safety at the March 31, 2018 Phoenix Summit. The summit known as the We the People Summit held at the Phoenix Convention Center was open to the public. It was comprised of twenty classes with topics including among others; Get Out the Vote, Youth and Activism, Arizona Elections, and Gun Violence Beyond the Rhetoric. In our address, we gave some commonsense gun safety ideas, especially from a mental health viewpoint. The audience, about fifty or so, was concerned teachers, parents, college students, and even members of the NRA. Panel members included an expert professor from Arizona State University, a student who was shot and almost died, an African American minister who does a lot of work in the inner city, and Sue and me.

Our turn to speak was last. We were the first people in the Arizona Gun Safety Association to interweave mental health and gun safety, according to the association's President. Sue started out with a review of the Nick Iorio story and how it devastated our family. This was the first time we could talk about the gun that was used in 1997 to take our son's life. In the past, we could talk about his suicide but not about the gun. While she was talking, I could see the tears flowing from many of the people in the audience. The message was powerful. She pointed out that the country needs to recognize that mental illness is a medical problem that affects all ages and all people but especially the young. Suicide might occur when a person becomes desperate. The person may feel like this is the only way out. Tragically, two-thirds of the 5,000 plus teens who take their lives by suicide each year use a gun from their home (The Jason Foundation, 2016). Sue concluded by stating that there is help from the American Foundation for Suicide Prevention (AFSP) and the National Suicide Prevention Lifeline. One of her main points was, if your child or loved one is suffering, get medical help and counseling right away. The right medication is paramount. And learn the signs of mental illness, which may include "feeling the blues" for a long period of time, agitation and anger all of the time, not being able to focus or sleep, or manic behavior.

I talked about how we were not coming from left or right or as Democrats or Republicans. Our goal has been to do the right thing. With that, I began to review other potential solutions to the mental illness and gun safety issues. People such as teachers, persons who sell guns, NRA members, professionals in business, parents, and other members of a community need to be educated. Media campaigns with community support exist, such as the AFSP Out of The Darkness Walk held each year in many communities nationwide.

In my interviews of many people over the last few years, they are starting to recognize that mental health disorders are indeed a medical problem and that guns are taking more lives particularly by suicide. I also discussed my own experience in corporate America, developing Employee Assistance Programs (EAP) to train managers and employees on how to recognize mental health issues, behaviors, and things that are not normal with a person. The key is to get that person help through an EAP. I heard many success stories with EAP intervention. Very few persons in the audience had EAP experience. One of my foremost points was that those with guns in their home NEED TO LOCK THEM UP or put them far away from their kids or grandkids or anyone else for that matter.

CONCLUSION

WHAT DOES IT ALL MEAN?

> "Let nothing frighten you...
> Who has God, lacks nothing."
> (St. Teresa Arvilla, Mark Link, *Vision 2000*,
> Tabor Publishing, 1992)

Our purpose in writing this book is to help people who have lost a child to suicide, or any human being for that matter. We discuss how we dealt with the grief associated with suicide, how we were able to move forward to enjoy life again, and how mental health, suicide, and gun safety play into the overall picture.

An important part of our story is how, with the help of our faith and Penn State, our family continued to live after Nick's death. It includes the Joe Iorio story, his rise in football at Penn State and the NFL, when so many said he could not do it. And it includes the Tim Iorio story, who after years of medical school, residency, and fellowship became a successful orthopedic surgeon. Sue and I survived and gave Tim and Joe love and support. We moved forward in our careers and learned to laugh and enjoy life again. And, of course, having grandkids is a blessing. Now that we are older, we find the strength to reflect on the worst time of our lives and to share our story.

Regarding mental health, it is imperative that you get your loved one help if you notice some change in his/her behavior, as described in this book. Contact your primary care doctor for a referral to a licensed and board-certified psychiatrist if you notice or are concerned about your loved one's change in behavior. It may take several visits, but the psychiatrist will make a diagnosis. Unless there is a physiological reason, mental illnesses are not usually diagnosed by an x-ray, scan, or a blood test like other diseases and are only visible on the outside. Counseling will be important, as well as providing a high amount of maintenance. By maintenance, we mean you must be aware where your loved one is at all times. This was the hardest part with Nick. Although he transferred to BGSU, only twenty minutes away from our home, it wasn't until his funeral that we discovered he did not get much sleep. So, besides being on the wrong medication and drinking alcohol, as many college students do, he was not sleeping. All of these things were disastrous. Do we wonder if we did enough? Yes, we wonder that all the time. However, we relied on our faith and the grace of God to see us through this human limitation.

The final point that we would like to make concerning mental illness is: there is HOPE! Life with mental illness is a tough journey. We are all in this together. Research in mental health has made many strides since the loss of our son, but there is still much to learn. The thing that still concerns us is the continued stigma concerning mental health and suicide. Although that aspect has improved somewhat, it still remains. Our belief is that mental illness is a medical problem, just like any other medical problem. Suicide can strike anyone or any family. Like Tim (Jr.) asked in a *The Toledo Blade* article on November 15, 1997, "Why our family?" There really is, again, no answer to this, except that tragedy and suffering are part of the human condition. Proverbs in the Holy Bible states, "Do not lean on your own understanding." It is still hard.

As for gun safety, we admire former Ohio Governor John Kasich's commonsense approach. We do not believe that all guns should be taken away from our citizens. However, the Colt AR 15 is questionable. We need compromise between all concerned parties with respect to the Colt AR 15s and perhaps other semi-automated guns. (This is a sensitive issue to gun owners; we understand.) There is evidence that the NRA does have a gun-safety policy. The NRA is concerned about gun safety and mental health. Its stance on Second Amendment rights is a strong one. Condoleezza Rice, former secretary of state, has argued that the Second Amendment is indeed an important provision in the United States Constitution; however, it needs to be reviewed in our modern world (Chasmar, February 23, 2018, *Washington Post*).

Let us conclude by stating it is all about saving lives. If this memoir has helped in any way, we are thankful to God! We are still hopeful and confident that strides will continue to be made in mental health, suicide prevention, and gun safety. President John F. Kennedy challenged Americans in his inaugural address, "Ask not what your country can do for you, ask what you can do for your country" (January 21, 1961). That certainly applies in the areas of mental health and gun safety. This will continue to be our mission in this life, to work for the good of our beloved country! May all citizens join together in this important cause. And, as President Kennedy and his brother, Bobby Kennedy, were quoted many times: "Some see things as they are and ask 'Why?' I dream of things that never were and ask, 'Why not?'" (The Kennedys adopted this phrase from George Bernard Shaw, *Time Special Edition, 50 Years Later*, Robert F. Kennedy, 2018.) That is our mantra: "Why not?"

Today, Joe is married to a wonderful woman, Nikki Peters. Together they live in Arizona with their two boxers, Diesel and Ridley, and baby Trent Nicolas, who was born on May 8, 2019. Tim and his lovely wife Tara and their three children, Tad, Reese, and Beckett, live in Columbus, Ohio, where Tim is practicing medicine as a hand surgeon. Currently, we live in Scottsdale, Arizona, near Joe and Nikki. I am working as an adjunct professor while continuing to provide consulting services, and Sue works part-time as a nurse practitioner.

Because of the busyness of life, we don't ask questions as much today on the why of losing Nick. The holidays, his birthday on February 11, and his anniversary on October 28 are still very painful. But we have accepted the reality of living without him.

EPILOGUE

One of the most difficult things that hit us has been the depression we have faced in losing Nick. Even though it has been more than twenty-two years since his death, there are times when we are thrown back into depression over losing him. I suspect that will continue the rest of our lives. I often remember what a prominent businessman once told me, "If you do not take care of yourself, no one else will." Sue and I continue to remind one another of this and help each other when those times return. Sometimes it requires medical help to overcome the depression. A chemical imbalance causing depression can recur after one suffers a tragic loss such as the loss of a child or a close loved one.

Made in the USA
Monee, IL
25 March 2021